Kalimba So

How to Play 100 Songs, from Classic to Modern on the Kalimba

Introduction

Are you a music lover who has developed a keen interest in playing the Kalimba?

Are you also looking for a comprehensive guide on how to play any song, whether classic or modern, on the Kalimba?

If you have answered yes to the above questions, read on because this book has a lot in store for you.

The Kalimba is a simple musical instrument that is fast becoming very popular due to its simplicity and unique sound. Thus, the Kalimba is among the best instruments a beginner could ask for, as you can easily learn to play it all independently.

Therefore, if you have the following questions;

- How do I teach myself the Kalimba?

- What are the techniques of playing the Kalimba?

- What can I learn about the Kalimba keys and notes?

And many others, then this book has you covered.

This book will comprehensively cover:

- What the Kalimba is

- How to tune and play the Kalimba

- How to read the Kalimba sheet music

- And popular songs to play on the Kalimba

So why wait! Flip over to the next page and get started in your journey to becoming a Kalimba master!

PS: I'd like your feedback. If you are happy with this book, please leave a review on Amazon.

Please leave a review for this book on Amazon by visiting the page below:

https://amzn.to/2VMR5qr

Table of Contents

Chapter 1: Basics of a Kalimba

The Kalimba is a simple musical instrument made using a wooden soundboard (mostly) and has steel keys that you play by plucking or strumming.

The Kalimba produces a soothing bell-like sound, mainly because it's based on a traditional African instrument from Zimbabwe called the Mbira. The Mbira, however, had a double row of keys compared to the single row of keys on the Kalimba.

Hugh Tracey was the man who created the Kalimba in the 1960s after hearing the sounds of Mbira while living in Zimbabwe. However, since he could not transfer Western music notes to the Mbira, he created the Kalimba, scaled to play western music.

Parts of the Kalimba

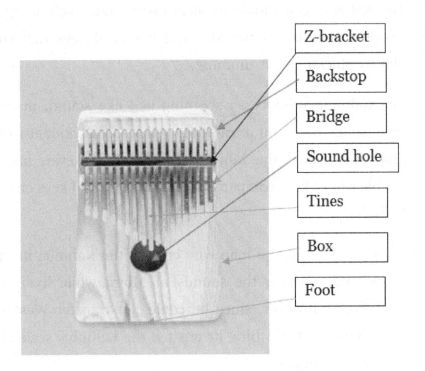

Let us now look at the parts of the Kalimba:

- **Body or Soundbox** – The body or soundboard of the Kalimba is the instrument's primary frame. The soundboard is where all the other parts of the Kalimba attach. The Kalimba box is usually comfortable to hold and play with both hands.

- **Soundhole** – The soundhole helps improve the sound resonance and project the sound a little louder, just like it does on the guitar. However, some Kalimbas will not have the soundhole but will still sound fine. Furthermore, other Kalimbas will have two smaller soundholes at the back for the same purpose.

- **Metal tines** – The Metal tines are the long metal keys of the Kalimba. They are the only moveable parts of the Kalimba and thus, should be made from durable metal. You play these tines with your thumbs, either by plucking or strumming.

- **Bridge** – The bridge is a rounded piece of metal that sits on top of another wooden block on the soundboard. Its function is to improve the resonance of the Kalimba.

- **Z bracket** – The Z bracket is a z-shaped piece of metal used to attach the metal tines to the soundboard.

- **Backstop** – This is a piece of tonewood above the z bracket that helps absorb the forces on the tines when you pluck, improving the sound. See, when you pluck the tines, you apply force. The force spreads across the whole metal to the top end. The backstop absorbs this force. Without it, the tines would rattle when you plucked the Kalimba.

- **Head and foot–** The head is the top edge of the Kalimba, while the foot is the bottom edge. In most Kalimbas, the head and foot have no direct role in how the instrument produces sound. However, some modern kalimbas put audio slots on the foot where you can attach an amplifier.

Chapter 2: Tuning the Kalimba

While the Kalimba is a simple instrument to play, an important step in taking full advantage of its unique sounds is to tune it before starting to play. This sounds like a complicated process, but it really is simple.

First, before looking at tuning your Kalimba, you can download a kalimba key chart. If you have the 10-key Kalimba, then its key chart will look like this:

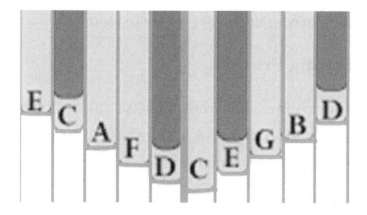

For the 17-key Kalimba, its key chart will look like this:

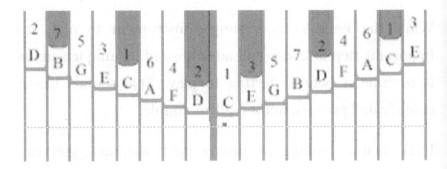

The key charts show you the notes on each key on your Kalimba. Thus, when tuning, you will be confirming whether the keys align with the notes it ought to represent.

The Tuning Process

Download a tuner. You can purchase simple tuners like Cleartune or VITALtuner, which are meant for guitars but will work fine for your Kalimba

Once you have your tuner, turn it on and place it next to your Kalimba. Also, have your key chart with you. You can mark the key notations on top of the metal tines with a marker for easier reference.

1. Then, begin by plucking the centermost tine as you look at the tuner on your phone. On the 17-note Kalimba, the longest tine will often be a C note. When

you pluck it then, you will see the needle of your tuner move and lock at C as soon as the sound is made. The same is true for the 10-note Kalimba, but it can also be a G. If you get either C or G on the 10-note Kalimba, it is well-tuned.

2. Go from one key to another and see if the tuner picks up sounds from eh key corresponding with what is on the key chart.

3. If you find a note out of place, you can use a simple tuning hammer to tune the note into place. For example, if the key chart says a key is C, but when you pluck it, the tuner says the key is a C flat (Cb), you will need to adjust the key upwards from a C flat to just C. Lightly tap the bottom of that key with your hammer to push it upwards a little. Please don't use too much force; give it light taps, then pluck until it gets to C.

4. On the other hand, if a note reads C sharp (C#) or D instead of C, then it means the note needs lowering.s So, you will now tap the top of the tine to push the note downwards. Keep tapping and checking the note

until it corresponds with what is on the key chart. Do this for every note on the Kalimba.

Once done, it is now ready to be played.

Playing the Kalimba

Playing the Kalimba is rather straightforward. Unlike instruments such as piano, where you have dozens of keys and complex scales and chords to get through, the Kalimba is straightforward. If you are a fast learner, you could get a hint of musical melody from your Kalimba within days.

Here is how to play the Kalimba:

Step 1:

Hold the Kalimba with both hands, with the metal tines facing you. Your thumbs should be at the top of the Kalimba, while the rest of your fingers should wrap around and behind the Kalimba. Your fingers shouldn't cover the two holes at the back.

Step 2:

Hit a tine with your thumb to make a sound. For the best sound, flick the tine with your thumbnail. This will make the tine vibrate, producing a melodic bell-like sound.

Since you do not have any notes to play, practice just hitting the tines so that your fingers get used to the motions. The tines will be painful on your thumbs, but after playing for a long time, your fingernails will get used to it.

You can also try a 3-finger style, where you pluck as you would with your thumbs and try plucking with the index finger. However, this will limit the finger to one or two notes on either side (left or right, depending on which index finger you choose). But, this opens up many possibilities.

One, you will cover a great distance across the instrument without having to put a strain on your thumbs. Second, you will be able to quickly play chords in succession if one of the chords is to the extreme end of the instrument. Rather than moving your thumb across, you can use the index finger to play the chord.

Another technique could be, rather than trying to pluck or strum all the notes, you can strum one note then pluck the next note if you are playing neighboring notes together. For example, if you are playing the 17-key Kalimba, E and G are next to each other. Thus, you could strum E, meaning you slide your finger down the tine to get sound, but then pluck G from beneath in the same motion. This technique reduces thumb movement and allows you to play for much longer without feeling like your thumbs are getting tired.

Step 3:

Alternate between both thumbs as you experiment with different notes on both sides of the Kalimba. Remember, a

Kalimba comes set in a specific key. Therefore, you won't get any wrong notes on it.

That said, now that you know how to hold the Kalimba and pluck it, how about getting down to learning how to read the Kalimba tab and getting to play songs on it.

Chapter 3: Kalimba Sheet Music – How to Read the Kalimba Tablature

Once you have learned your notes and practiced enough for your finger to get used to the Kalimba, it is time to get down to learning the Kalimba Tab. Learning the Kalimba Tab is critical if you want to play specific songs on the Kalimba.

The Kalimba tab is a sheet music representation of how you ought to play the Kalimba to achieve certain melodic tunes or hit certain notes. The Kalimba Tab offers you the best way to learn new songs on the Kalimba.

It is often represented as elongated Kalimba metal tines and shows you exactly the tine you need to pluck/strum to play the song you want.

Below is how a Kalimba tab looks. The tab is for the 17-Key Kalimba, and as you see, the Kalimba tab also has 17-keys.

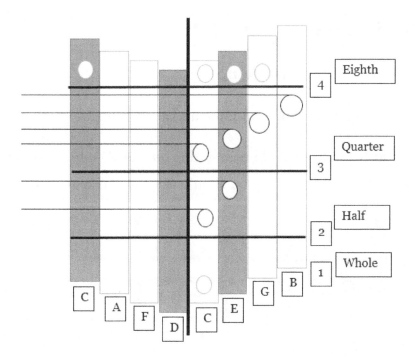

On the Kalimba tablature, you will also see notations represented by letters.

Reading the Kalimba Tab

How to play a single note

Below is a diagram of a Kalimba and a Kalimba tab.

On the Kalimba tab, there is a dot on the C note. The dot represents the note that you should play in that sequence.

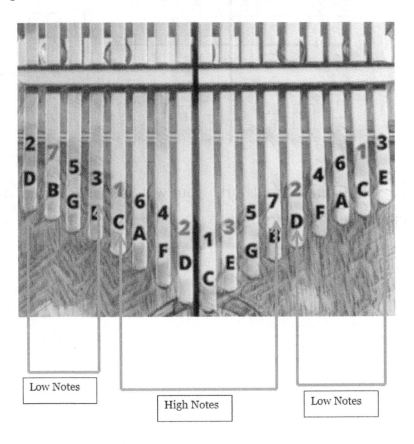

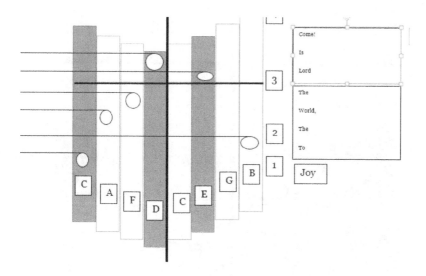

If the dots are arranged one higher than the other, the one lowest is the one you will play first, followed by the second-lowest, and so on. The one with the highest dot will go last, as we will see when learning to play a melody.

Playing a Chord

In music, you create a chord when you play up to three notes at the same time. The diagram below shows the Kalimba tab showing three dots on the same line, which means we will play all three notes at once, C-E-G. You can play them by sliding your finger across the three metal tines.

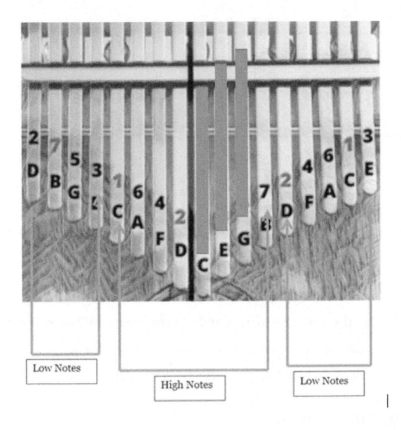

Low Notes

High Notes

Low Notes

However, note that you won't always have to play chords on the same side. Sometimes, you will have to play two notes at the same time on both sides of the Kalimba. This is why it is important to practice before trying to learn how to play a song —so that your thumbs become more flexible to play two notes at the same time.

Playing Melodies

Next is learning how to play notes one after another to create a melody. The diagram below shows that the notes C-E-G have dots rising from each note.

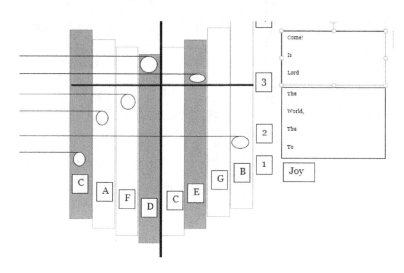

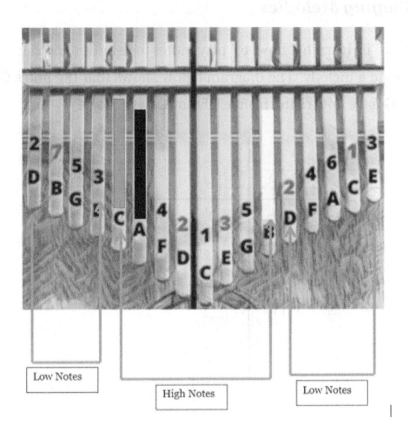

This means we will play note C first and finish with G.

Numbered and Lettered Notations

Sometimes, it can be quite hard to represent a song on a Kalimba well on paper, especially for beginners. This is where the numbered and lettered notations come in.

Rather than showing you the Kalimba tablature, the numbered and lettered notations write down the notes you should play with either letters or numbers.

Now, we all know the sofa ladder music notes – do, re, mi, fa, so, la, ti. These seven notes are the ones represented by numbers or letters. Therefore, do, re, mi, fa, so, la, ti as a numbered notation will be 1 2 3 4 5 6 7. As a lettered notation meanwhile, it will be C D E F G A B.

On the 17 note Kalimba, it will be as shown below.

C	D	E	F	G	A	B	C'	D'	E'	F'	G'	A'	B'	C"	D"	E"
1	2	3	4	5	6	7	1	2	3	4	5	6	7	1	2	3

A plain note represents a quarter note or crotchet. The one with a dot represents a quaver or an eighth of a note. Two dots make the note a semiquaver or a sixteenth of a note.

When playing the 17-note Kalimba, the Centre is C. To play half notes, you will pluck the tines on the right, while the tines on the left will be whole notes.

Numbered and lettered notations are useful for beginners because they allow notes to line up with the song lyrics. For some, this is a more convenient way of learning how to play a new song on the Kalimba.

Consider the example below of a numbered notation

of Twinkle Twinkle Little Star.

1 1 5 5 6 6 5

Twin-kle twin-kle Lit-tle star

44 33 221

How I wond-der what you are

Notice how much simpler it appears than how it looks on the Kalimba tab below.

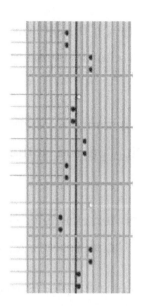

Lettered notations also perform the same function. Below is an example of Twinkle Twinkle Little Star as a lettered notation.

C C   G G AA G   F   FE E D   D   C

Twinkle, Twinkle little star. How I wonder what you are.

G F   F E   E D   G   G F F   E E   D

Up above the world so high, Like a diamond in the sky.

C C   G G AA G   F   FE E D   D   C

Twinkle, Twinkle little star. How I wonder what you are.

Now, you might wonder, if this is how one represents single notes, then how is a chord represented in numbered and lettered notations?

Well, a chord in this instance is often represented in one of three ways, depending on the author's preference of the music.

1. Using brackets; for example, when notes are shown as (135) or (CEG), representing a chord.

2. Using dashes, for example, 1-3-5 or C-E-G is a chord.

3. Stacking the numbers or letters on top of one another.

However, the third style is less common than the first two.

Adding Effects to How You Play the Kalimba

While the Kalimba already sounds great on its own, there are additional techniques you can use to add some effects to the instrument's sound. You can practice these once you're well on your way to mastering playing the Kalimba notes.

The 'Wah-wah' effect

The wah-wah effect has nothing to do with how you pluck or strum the metal tines and everything to do with how you use the soundhole at the front of your Kalimba (assuming you are using the standard Kalimba with the soundhole).

To create the wah-wah effect, you will need to be dexterous with your thumbs as you will pluck with one thumb while closing the soundhole with the other. You will also change thumbs depending on where you are playing the notes.

Typically, only about three or four notes in the mid-range of the Kalimba will strongly be affected by the wah-wah effect. Experiment with the instrument - pluck each note as you cover the soundhole with your thumb to see which one gets strongly affected by the effect. Often, you will find the notes towards the center (longer tines) get more affected than the shorter ones.

Glissando effect

The glissando effect is another simple yet effective way of making the Kalimba sound much more pleasant. If you have ever listened to a harp, when the harp player strums several strings at once, then you have listened to the glissando effect.

To do the glissando effect on the Kalimba, you start from the center, touch a tine with your thumb, and then slide the thumb across the other tines.

When you slide your thumb across three adjacent tines, you create a triad. When you slide across four tines, you create a 7th chord, and when you slide across five, you create a 9th chord.

At first, it will be much harder to complete the glissando effect smoothly, but you should be able to do it with time. To perform the effect better, keep your thumbnail a little longer so that you can use the tip of the nail to slide across the tines.

Once you get better, you can perform the outside-in effect, starting from the outside tines towards those at the center.

The Vibrato effect

You will need to have a Kalimba with two holes at the back to create this effect. If your Kalimba has two holes on the side, it can still work.

To perform the vibrato effect, cover and uncover these two holes. This action changes the tonal properties of the notes you play.

The Staccato effect

Whenever you pluck a tine, the sound will often vibrate for some time after you pluck. However, sometimes, you might want to stop the sound immediately. So, how do you achieve this?

After plucking a tine, touch it with the back of your thumb to completely stop the tine. This is what is called the staccato effect.

While practicing, also practice how to play the Kalimba at different volume levels. Now, the Kalimba doesn't have a volume up or down button. However, the pressure you put on the tines determines how loud or low the sound is.

Therefore, practice different ways to pluck the Kalimba r to get different volume levels on the instrument. This is important because it helps you recreate the trickier parts of a song, for example, when the instruments play more softly or more loudly.

Having looked at how to play the Kalimba, let's now look at some classic and modern great songs you can recreate with your Kalimba

Chapter 4: Classic Songs You Can Play on the Kalimba

This chapter will highlight some of the most popular songs you can play on the Kalimba, stretching from the old classics to modern-day pop songs. The stretch of these songs speaks volumes of the versatility of the Kalimba – simple yet astonishingly multi-faceted.

This chapter looks at some classic and modern songs you can play quite easily on the Kalimba.

Classic Songs to Play on the Kalimba

Classic songs have a lasting worth or quality even though they may be old.

There are several classic songs you can play on the Kalimba. Below, we look at some of them and how to play them.

1: *Jingle Bells*

Jingle Bells is a very well-known classic that will forever remain in the psyche of any generation as long as Christmas remains.

The song was written by James Lord Pierpont around 1857. Since then, it has been associated with Christmas, especially with Santa and his sleigh. This is despite Lord Pierpont having meant it as a song for Thanksgiving and not Christmas.

But the song remains a favorite today. On the Kalimba, here is how you will play the song:

E E E   E E E   E G C D E

Jingle bells, jingle bells, jingle all the way,

F F   F FFE E EE

oh, what fun it is to ride in a

E D   D E D G

one-horse open sleigh.

E E E   E E E   E G C D E

Jingle bells, jingle bells, jingle all the way,

F F   F FFE E EE

oh, what fun it is to ride in a

G   G   F D C

one-horse open sleigh.

2: *Soft Kitty*

You have heard of the Soft Kitty lullaby if you are familiar with the very popular sitcom, The Big Bang Theory. The show brought the traditional folk song to the fore of many people's minds in the modern age by having Penny sing it to Sheldon.

However, the song is very old and originally written by Edith Newling. It was first published in 1937 in a book called 'Songs for The Nursery School' and is only two sentences long. But that did not stop the song from selling over 10,000 copies, which, in 1937, was quite a feat.

The song is one of the easiest songs you will ever play in the Kalimba. Below are the song notes.

D BBCA A GAB CD

Soft Kit-ty, warm kit-ty, lit-tle ball of fur

D DB BC CAAA GA

Hap-py kit-ty, slee-py kit-ty, purr purr purr.

3: Old MacDonald Had a Farm

First published around 1917, this old nursery rhyme is a popular song worldwide. However, the song's history goes back further to around 1908, when the song "'Workhouse Marlebone' a rest home in London" was discovered in London. This song was believed to have been the inspiration for Old MacDonald.

The song's author remains unknown, but it was originally sung by an old lady called Mrs. Goodey, who sang hers based on another American song called 'Ohio.'

But the origins of the song aside, there is little doubt that Old MacDonald is a timeless classic that we have all had the pleasure of singing in our early days in school.

Here is how you will play it on the Kalimba.

CCCGAA GEED DC

Old MacDonald had a farm, E-I-E-I-O.

GCC C G A A G EED DC

And on his farm, he had some chicks, E-I-E-I-O.

GG C C CGG C c c

With a chick, chick here, and a chick, chick there. cc c

CCC ccccc

Here a chick, there a chick, everywhere a chick, chick,

CCC GAA GEED DC C

Old MacDonald had a farm, E-I-E-I-O.

4: Incy Wincy Spider

Ah, who can forget the timeless classic that sings about many people's pathological fears!

Incy Wincy Spider was a song whose origins are not yet known. However, sources attribute it to a song for adults named 'Camps and Camino' whose main words were 'blooming, bloody' rather than 'incy wincy.' However, the song was first published in 1920 and, throughout the years, has seen its lyrics vary according to region.

The title aside, the song speaks about not giving up. The incy wincy spider gets beaten down by the rain but still manages to wait for the sun and come out to play.

The song is very easy to play on the Kalimba, especially because, at most, it has five notes for you to play.

G CC C D E E.E DC DE C

The Incy Wincy spider climbed up the water spout.

E EFG G F EFGE

Down came the rain, and washed the spider out

CCDEE D C DE C

Out came the sun, and dried up all the rain.

G GCC CD EE E D C D EC

And the incy wincy spider climbed up the spout

again.

5: *Mary Had a Little Lamb*

Yet another timeless classic, this song was composed by Lowell Martin and was based on a real-life person called Mary Elizabeth Sawyer. Mary, born in 1806, on a farm in Scotland, had a pet lamb she loved.

The song has a simple melody that makes it very easy to pick up and can be a great beginning to practice your kalimba playing skills. It has a soft, relaxing melody, making it a great lullaby for your child after a long day.

This is an even simpler song, with only three notes – E D C– to play

Mary had a little lamb

EDCDEEE

Little lamb, little lamb

DDDEGG

Mary had a little lamb

EDCDEEE

Its fleece was white as snow

EDDEDC

And everywhere that Mary went

EDCDEEE

Mary went, Mary went

DDDEGG

Everywhere that Mary went

EDCDEEE

The lamb was sure to go

EDDEDC

He followed her to school one day

EDCDEEE

School one day, school one day

DDDEGG

He followed her to school one day

EDCDEEE

Which was against the rule

EDDEDC

It made the children laugh and play

EDCDEEE

Laugh and play, laugh and play

DDDEGG

It made the children laugh and play

EDCDEEE

To see a lamb at school

EDDEDC

And so the teacher turned him out

EDCDEEE

Turned him out, turned him out

DDDEGG

And so the teacher turned him out

EDCDEEE

But still he lingered near

EDDEDC

And waited patiently

EDCDEEE

Patiently, patiently

DDDEGG

And wai-aited patiently

EDCDEEE

Til Mary did appear

EDDEDC

6: Birthday Song

The 'Happy Birthday' song has become one of the most famous songs, and most people have sung it at least once in their lives.

The song has been recreated in every language imaginable, and many artists have made renditions of it.

Its origins remain a mystery, though. However, the melody dates back to 1893, with the original song called 'good morning to all.' The song composers were two American Sisters, Patty Hill and Mildred.

However, it wasn't until 1912 that the song was remade, with 'Happy Birthday to you' as the lyrics. The song has six notes for you to play, but it is rather straightforward and is a song you should play quite easily.

Below is a numbered and lettered notation of the song.

G GAG CB

5 5 6 5 1 7

Hap-py birth-day to you

G GA GDC

5 5 6 5 2 1

hap-py birth-day to you.

GGGE C BA

5 5 5 3 1 7 6

Hap-py birth-day dear (persons name)

F FEC DC

4 4 3 1 2 1

hap-py birth-day to you.

Now, aside from nursery rhymes, we can also get classics made by prominent artists and famous singers during their time.

Below are some songs that topped charts during their time and are still widely played today.

Note that while the above nursery rhymes classics will be perfectly played on a 10-key Kalimba alone, having the 17-key Kalimba will serve you best to play the songs below.

7: *We Wish You a Merry Christmas*

We begin this segment with yet another Christmas song. The beauty of Christmas songs is that they are such obvious classics because they get played yearly without fail. Thus, almost everyone is familiar with them.

We wish you a Merry Christmas is often accredited to Arthur Warrell, though history dictates that the song was composed way back in the 1500s. The song's original meaning was of servants threatening their masters as they demanded more wine and food.

However, Warrell made his own arrangement for the song for his University of Bristol Madrigal Singers, which he performed as 'A Merry Christmas: We Wish You a Merry Christmas' in a concert on December 6, 1935.

On the Kalimba, the song is fairly easy to play, as shown below.

G C C DC BA A

We wish you a me-rry Christ-mas

ADDED C B|G

We wish you a me-rry Christ-mas

GEE FED C A G GA DB C

We wish you a me-rry Christ-mas and a hap-py new year

G CC CB BC BAG

Good ti-dings we bring to you and your kin

GE D DC C G G G G A D B C

We wish you a me-rry Christ-mas and a hap-py new year

8: What a Wonderful World

This song was composed by Louis Armstrong, a famous jazz soloist and considered one of the most influential musicians of all time. Indeed, his music has impacted jazz history soo much that many scholars, critics, and fans call him the greatest jazz soloist of all time.

What a Wonderful World is one of his most famous and beloved songs. The song speaks about the need to appreciate the beauty of your surroundings. Armstrong originally recorded the song in 1967; however, the song has been covered by many modern-day artists since then.

However, the original by Armstrong captures the emotions of the lyrics, and when played on the Kalimba, the song is a very laid-back, chilled tune.

C E F A C°
I see trees of green,

D° D°-D° C°
Red roses too

B B B A
I see them bloom,

G G G F
For me and you

F F F F F – F
And I think to myself,

F F E – F – G A
What a wonderful world.

C E F A C°
I see skies of blue,

D° D° D° C°

And clouds of white.

B B B A

The bright blessed day,

G G G – G F

The dark sacred night.

F F F F F – F

And I think to myself,

F F E – F – G F

What a wonderful world...

9: *Somewhere Over the Rainbow*

Yip Harburg wrote the original lyrics to this song. However, the song was sung by Judy Garland in 1939.

The song speaks of the need to maintain hope, remain optimistic, and believe that despite any setbacks currently, somewhere over the rainbow, dreams can come true.

However, the most famous rendition of this song was by Hawaiian singer Israel Kamakawiwo'ole or IZ in short, a song released in 1990. IZ made the song with beautiful, buoyant lyrics set to the backdrop of beautiful ukulele strums.

On the Kalimba, the song is rather easy to learn and play. Below is how you will play it on the Kalimba.

Number notes

Version 1

1° 1°° 7° 5° 6° 7° 1° 1° 6° 5°

1° 4° 3° 1° 2° 3° 4° 2° 7 1° 2° 3° 1°

5° 3° 5° 3° 5° 3° 5° 3°

5° 4° 5° 4° 5° 4° 5° 4°

5° 6° 6°

1° 43° 1° 2° 3° 4° 2° 7 1° 2° 3° 1°

5° 3° 5° 3° 5° 3° 5° 3°

5° 4° 5° 4° 5° 4° 5° 4°

5° 6° 6° 1° 5°|

Letter notes

Version 1

C° C B° G° A° B° C°° C° A° G°

C° F° E° C D E F° D° B C D° E° C°

G° E G E G° E° G° E°

G° F G° F G° F° G° F°

G°A°A°

C° FE° C D E F° D° B C D° E° C°

G° E° G° E° G° E° G° E°

G° F G F G° F° G° F°

G°A° A° C°° G°|

10: Imagine – John Lennon

John Lennon was one of the most popular artists of his time. As the lead guitarist of the world-famous boy band, *The Beatles,* John Lennon also had success as a solo artist and among his many hits is the song Imagine.

Lennon recorded and released the song in 1971, with the song getting featured in the movie, *Mr. Holland's Opus.*

It is a soft rock that John Lennon co-wrote with his wife, Yoko Ono, and was inspired by Lennon's atheistic approach to religion and Yoko Ono's reflections on her conceptual art. The song was number one in the UK charts on the year of its release and also re-entered the charts in 1981, peaking at number three.

On the Kalimba, the song is represented as both number and letter notes, as shown below, along with the lyrics.

53-53-53-53

GE-GE-GE-GE

64-64-64-64

AF-AF-AF-AF

6-7-1

A-B-C°

3 5 3577 6

E-G-EGBB-A

Imagine there's no heaven.

35 35 77⁶

EG-EGBB-A

It's easy if you try

357-7⁶3-535-77-⁶

EGB-BAE-GEG-B B-A

No hell below us, above us only sky...

616 13 3 2 16

A-C°-A C° E° E°-D°-C°-A

Imagine all the people

7 77¹ 2 353 ²¹

B-BBC-D E-G° E°-D°-C°|

Living for today

3-5-3577-6

E-G-EG BB-A

Imagine there's no countries,

35-35 77-6

E G-E G B B-A

It isn't hard to do

3-5 35776

E-GEGBBA

Nothing to kill or die for

35 3-5-77-6

EGE-G-B B-A

And no religion too...

61 6133216

A-C°-A C° E° E°-D°-C°-A

Imagine all the people

7771235321

B-BB C D E°-G°-E°-D°-C°

Living life in peace

717176671165

B C B-C BA A B C°-C°-A-G|

You may say I'm a dreamer ~

61776623

A C° BBA-A D-E

But I'm not the only one

66176671165

AAC-B-AA-B C° C°-A-G

I hope someday you'll join us ~

712321

B C° D°-E°-D°-C°

And the world ~

2311

D° E° C° C°

Will be as one!|

Elvis Presley

Elvis Presley gained the reputation of being the King of Rock 'n Roll. In his time, he was one of the most popular artists alive.

Two of his classics, *I Can't Help Falling in Love with You* and *Love Me Tender*, are great songs to play on the Kalimba.

11: I Can't Help Falling in Love with You

This was a song written by Hugo Peretti, George David Weiss, and Luigi Creatore. However, Elvis recorded the song for his album Blue Hawaii in 1961.

The song topped charts on the US Billboard, and the UK, Australia, Netherlands, and many other countries.

The song became so popular that many talented artists, including Haley Reinhart and Twenty One Pilots, have covered it.

The song sounds good on the Kalimba, and its notes are below.

C G C D E F E D

Wise men say, On-ly fools rush in

G A B C D E F E D C

But I can't help fall-ing in love with you

C G C D E F E D

Shall I stay? Would it be a sin

G A B C D E F E D C

If I can't help fall-ing in love with you?

B E G B A B E G B A

Like a riv-er flows, sure-ly to the sea

B E G B A

Dar-ling, so it goes

G G E G E F G

Some things are meant to be

C G C D E F E D

Take my hand, take my whole life too

G A

C   D   E   F   E   D   C

For I can't help fall-ing in love with you

12: *Love Me Tender*

Originally, this song was a civil war song published in 1861, composed by Aura Lee. However, it was originally only a melody, as it had no lyrics.

It wasn't until 1956 that Elvis Presley released the song as a love ballad with lyrics, and the song quickly became popular among the masses.

The song has become so popular that it has been used on multiple films and TV shows such as Die Hard 2, Wild at Heart, Touched by Love, This is Elvis and many others.

As shown below, the song is very relaxing and easy to play on the Kalimba.

G C° B C° D° A D°

Love me ten-der, love me sweet,

C° B A B C°

Ne-ver let me go.

G C° B C° D° A D°

You have made my life com-plete,

C° B A B C°

and I love you so.

E° E° E° E° E° E° E°

Love me ten-der, love me true.

E° D° C° D° E°

All my dreams fulfil,

E° E° F° E° D° A° D°

for my dar-lin I love you

C° B A B C°

and I al-ways will.

Johnny Cash

Johnny Cash was an American singer considered one of the most important artists in music history. His songs were so popular that they have been replayed countless times over in various instruments.

We look at two of his most popular songs.

13: *You Are My Sunshine*

While not originally Johnny Cash's, his version is the most famous. The song was a lullaby that became popular in 1939 when Cash was about 7.

The song is one of the best-known songs in history and is great to play slowly, especially as a beginner. It is a calming and relaxing tune that will sound great on the Kalimba.

G C D E E   E DE C C

You are my sunshine, my only sunshine.

C D   E FA A   G   F E

You make me happy when skies are grey.

C   DE F   A A   G   F E C

You'll never know dear, how much I love you.

C   D   E   F D D   E C

Please don't take my sunshine away.

14: Hurt

Once again, the song was not a "Johny Cash original," but by an American Rock Band called Nine Inch Nail in 1995.

However, it became extremely popular after Johnny Cash covered it in 2002. While the original had been about a young man on a downward spiral, Cash's rendition was about a man nearing the end of his life (Cash was suffering from autonomic neuropathy caused by diabetes). Thus, the song was a reflective piece of the life he had lived.

Below is how to play it on the Kalimba

I hurt myself today

3°5°3°2°1°3°

E G E D C E

To see if I still feel

5 1° 6 2°1°3°

G C A D C E

I focus on the pain

3° 5° 3° 2° 1° 3°

E G E D C E

The only thing that's real

5 1° 6 2° 5 6

G C A D G A

The needle tears a hole

3°5°3°2°1°3°

E G E D C E

The old familiar sting

5 1° 6 2° 1° 3°

G C A D C E

Try to kill it all away

3° 3° 5° 3° 2° 1° 3°

E E G E D C E

But I remember everything

5 1° 6 1° 1° 2° 5 6

G C A C C D G A

What have I become

5° 5° 3° 1° 1°

G G E C C

My sweetest friend?

1° 2° 1° 2°

C D C D

Everyone I know

5° 5° 3° 1° 1°

G G E C C

Goes away in the end

6 5 3° 3° 5 5

A G E E G G

And you could have it all

2° 2° 1° 3° 1° 1°

D D C E C C

My empire of dirt

2°2°2°52°

D D D|G D

I will let you down

2°1°3°1°1°

D C E C C

I will make you hurt

2°1°3°56

I wear this crown of thorns

3°5°3°2°1°3°

E G E D C E

Upon my liar's chair

5 1° 6 2° 1° 3°

G C|A D C E

Full of broken thoughts

5° 3° 2° 1° 3°

G E D C E

I cannot repair

1° 6 2° 5 6

C A D G A

Beneath the stains of time

3° 5° 3° 2° 1° 3°

E G E D C E

The feelings disappear

5 1° 6 2° 1° 3°

G C A D C E

You are someone else

5° 3° 2° 1° 3°

G E D C E

I am still right here

1° 6 2° 5 6

C A D G A

What have I become

5° 5° 3° 1° 1°

G G E C C

My sweetest friend?

1° 2° 1° 2°

C D C D

Everyone I know

5° 5° 3° 1° 1°

G E C C

Goes away in the end

6 5 3° 3° 5 5

A G E E G G

And you could have it all

2°2°1°3°1°1°

D D C E C C

My empire of dirt

2° 2° 2° 5 2°

D D D G D

I will let you down

2° 1° 3° 1° 1°

D C E C C

I will make you hurt

2° 1° 3° 5 6

D C E G A

could start again

2° 2° 1° 3° 1° 1°

D D C E C C

A million miles away

2° 2° 1° 3° 5 2°

D D C E G D

I will keep myself

2° 1° 3° 1° 1°

D C E C C

I would find a way

2° 1° 3° 5 6

D C E G A

15: Symphony No 5

Symphony No 5 is a magnificent composition by the great music composer Ledwig van Beethoven. Written between 1804 and 1808, the song is considered one of the best compositions in classical music.

While the song's start is dense and suspenseful, it grows into a jovial, electrifying feeling of positivity and joy. The chords of the music are quite easy to recreate on the Kalimba, as shown below.

6664

5553

6664

2° 2° 2° 6

4 4 4 2"

6665

3° 3° 3° 1°

5° 5° 5° 3°

6° 6° 5° 4°

6° 6° 5° 4°

6° 6° 5° 4° 2° 6°

6° 6° 6° 4°

5° 5° 5° 3°

6° 6° 6° 4°

2** 2** 2** 6°

4° 4° 4° 2°

6 6 6 5°

3** 3** 3** 2**

5° 5° 5° 3°

6° 6° 5° 4°

6° 6° 5° 4°

6° 6° 5° 4° 2° 6°

6° 6° 6° 5"

6° 6° 6° 5°

6° 6° 6° 5°

6° 6° 6° 2**

6° 6° 6° 2**

6° 6° 6° 2° 6° 2° 6° 2° 6° 2° 6°

2

6°

2|

Letter notes

AAAF

GGGE

AAAF

DDDA

FFFD

AAAG

EEEC

GGGE

AAGF

AAGF

AAGFDA

AAAF

GGGE

AAAF

D

DDA

FFFD

AAAG

E** E** E** D**

GGGE

AAGF

A A G F

A A G F D** A*

A A A G

A A A G

A A A G

A A A D**

A A A D

A A A D A D A D A D A

D

A

D|

A° A° A° G°

E°° E°° E°° D°°

G° G♭° G° E°

A° A° G° F°

A° A° G° F°

A° A° G° F° D°° A°

A° A° A° G°

A° A° A° G°

A° A° A° G°

A° A° A° D°°

A° A° A° D°°

A° A° A° D°° A° D°° A° D°° A°° D°° A°

D°°

A°

D°

16: Cinderella by Ilene Woods

Disney has gifted us with wonderful music over the years, music that has gone on to define an era. And this was true for its very first successful Cinderella movie.

The Cinderella song was performed by then 18-year-old Ilene Woods in 1948 during the recording of the movie. This was the song where Cinderella and the Prince sang as they fell in love.

The song's melody is mellow and makes it quite a compelling song that details how it is like to fall in love. The song makes your heart flutter and stomach knot pleasantly as it would when around your loved one. No doubt then, these gentle melodic qualities make it a great piece of music for the Kalimba.

Number notes

565 (16)

(35)5 6 5 (16) 356

565 (26) 4 (261°) (457)

5 (11) 3 (572°) (51°) (37) 5 (72°) 51° (246) 5 43 432

67 6 (2457)

5676 (257)

45 7 6 7 6 (357) (4|72°) (61°) (457)

' 2° 7 (61) (25) (47) (42°) (24°) 4 (72°5°) 5 (72°) (131°3°)

3°° 2° 1° 7° 6°5° 3°

35 65 (16)

(351 3°) 5 6 5 (16) 3 5 (61°3°) 5 6 5 (246)

2° 6° 4° 3° 4° 3°2°2° 7 6 55

(13°5°) 2 (35°) 4 (55°)

11°3°5°) 3 (572°4°) 3 5 (73°) (26) 4 6 2° 4° 3° (2462°4°)

6 (26) 4 (57) 4 (61°)

(23°) 4 (572°) 5

7 (13) (15) 35 (1°3°) (35°) 3° (57) 565 (26)

4 5 6 5 (26) 4 5 2° 5 (246) (573°) (131°) (13)

Letter notes

GAG (CA)

(EG)G A G (CA) EGA

GAG (DA) F (DAC) (FGB)

G (CC°) E (GBD°) (GC°) (EB) G (BD°)

GC° (DFA) G F EFED

ABA (DFGB) GABA (DGB)

FG BABA (EGB) (FBD) (AC) (FGB)

F° D° B (AC°) (DG) (FB) (FD°) (DF°) F (BD°G°) G (BD)
(CEC E°)

E** D** C** B* A*G* E*

EG AG (CA)

(EGC°E°) G A G (CA) E G (AC°E) GAG (DFA) D°°A° F° E°
F° E°D'D' BAGG

(CE°G°) D (EG°) F (GG°)

(CC°E°G°) E (GBD°F°) E G (BE°) (DA) FA D° F° E°
(DFAD°F°)

A (DA) F (GB) F (AC°)

(DE°) F (GBD°) G

B (C°E°) (CG°) E G (C°E°) (EG°) E° (GB) GAG (DA)

FGAG (DA) F G D G (DFA) (GBE°) (CEC) (CE)

17: *I'd Like to Teach the World to Sing*

This song originally came from a jingle in an advert. The song was produced by Billy Davis and performed by the Hillside Singers for the Coca-Cola company in 1971.

Despite being an advert, the song would soon become a smash hit, with people across the United States requesting DJs to play the song. The Coca-Cola Company also reported improved sales after the song's release, improving its popularity across the world.

The song remains popular, uniting both the old and new generations. The gentle jingle is perfect for the Kalimba, with straightforward notes for you to play with relative ease.

A G A C   A G   A C   A   D   E   D   E   D

I'd like to build the world a home, and fur-nish it with love.

E   D E   G   E   D   E G   E   C   D   C   A G

Grow ap-ple trees and hon-ey-bees and snow-white tur-tle doves.

A G   A   D   A   G   A C   A D E   D   E   D

I'd like to teach the world to sing In pe-rfect har-mo-ny.

E   D   E   G   E D   E G   E   C   D C   A C

I'd like to hold it in my arms, and keep it com-pa-ny.

18: Streets of London

When we talk of songs singing praise for cities, it doesn't get any better than Ralph Mctell, who wrote and sang the song released in 1969.

Ralf's soft voice takes you on tour through the streets of London, showing you what goes on in everyday life in the England capital. The song peaked at Number 2 in the UK charts and was re-recorded in 2017 to reflect a more modern London.

With a soft melody, the song is ideal for the Kalimba. Though it is slightly more complex than other songs, especially because you have to time how to repeat the notes, it is still a song that you can play well with enough practice.

E   E   E   E   G G   E D   C   C   E   E

Have you seen the old man in the closed-down mar-ket?

A   A   A   C   C   C   C   D   D E D

Kick-ing up the papers with his worn-out shoes.

E   E   E   G   G   G G   C   C   B   C E F   E

In his eyes, you see no pride, hand-held loose-ly by his side.

A   A   C   C   C   C C   G A   B   C

Yes-ter-day's pa-per tel-ling ye-ster-day's news.

Bob Dylan

Bob Dylan is a prominent American singer regarded as one of the greatest songwriters. He has been a prominent figure in pop culture for almost 60 years, with most of his songs considered classics.

Let us look at some of his songs that you can play on the Kalimba.

19: Blowin' in the Wind

Bob Dylan wrote this song in 1962 as part of the album *The Freewheelin' Bob Dylan*.

The song is a protest song, with Bob Dylan positing rhetorical questions about war, peace, and freedom. This then leads to the refrain, 'The answer, my friend, is blowin' in the wind.'

The folk song has a slow melody and will undoubtedly be simple to play on the Kalimba:

Letter notes

GABC° C°BA DGAB D°A D D°G

DGBC° C°BA AGFG

(GBD°) D°D°E° E°E°D° BAG

B (D°D) D°D° (E°E) D°C°D° DGDF

BC°(GBD°) D°D°E° E°E°D° BAG

B (D°D) D°B(C°C) C°BA DGDF

ABC° C°BA DFAB BB AG

EGBC° C°BA AG DFG

(GBD°) D°D°E° E°E°D° BAG

B (D°D) D°D° (E°E) D°C°D° DGDF

BC°(GBD°) D°D°E° E°E°D° BAG

B (D°D) D°B(C°C) C°BA DGDF

GABC° C°BA DGAB D°A D D°G

DGBC° C°BA AGFG

GABC° C°BA DGAB D°A D D°G

DGBC° C°BA AGFG

ABC° C°BA AG DFG

Number notation

5671° 1°76 2567 2°6 2 2°5

2571° 1°76 6545

(572°) 2°2°3° 3°3°2° 765

7 (2°2) 2°2° (3°3) 2°1°2° 2524

71°(572°) 2°2°3° 3°3°2° 765

7 (2°2) 2°7(1°1) 1°76 2524

671° 1°76 2467 77 65

1° 1°76 65 245

(572°) 2°2°3° 3°3°2° 765

7 (2°2) 2°2° (3°3) 2°1°2° 2524

71°(572°) 2°2°3° 3°3°2° 765

7 (2°2) 2°7(1°1) 1°76 2524

5671° 1°76 2567 2°6 2 2°5

2571° 1°76 6545

5671° 1°76 2567 2°6 2 2°5

2571° 1°76 6545

671° 1°76 65 245

20: Knockin' on Heaven's Door

Knockin' on Heaven's Door was released in 1973 and became one of Bob Dylan's most popular songs, reaching Top 10 in several countries.

The simple song has two short verses and was originally written as the soundtrack for the film *Pat Garret and Billy the Kid*. Indeed, the chorus is a comment directly to a scene in the film featuring one of the characters dying and has been making his last wishes, hence 'Knockin' on Heaven's Door.'

This is one of Bob Dylan's most covered compositions and is described as an 'exercise in simplicity.

The song features a strong guitar presence from Bob Dylan himself and his smooth fatherly vocals.

On the Kalimba, you cannot replicate Bob Dylan's voice, but you can recreate the song melody with relative ease.

BAG (A-C-E) BAGG (E-C) BAG (A-C-E) BAGG (E-C)

BBBBA AGA

BBAAGGE

GBBAA AGA

GBBAAAGGE

BBBBBAGA

BBBBBGGE

BBBBBA GA

BBBBBGGE

BBBBAA GA

BBAAGGE

GBBAAAGA

GBBAAAGGE

BBBBBAGA

BBBBBGGE

BBBBBAGA

BBBBBG GE

BAG (A-C-E) BAGG (E-C)

BAG (A-C-E) BAGG (E-C)|

Michael Jackson

Michael Jackson, or MJ as many so fondly call him, is justifiably referred to as the greatest performing artist of all time. Considering how his songs resonate as much with the young as with the old, it is hard to disagree. Jackson's lasting legacy means his songs are classic and modern.

However, in this section, we will look at his earlier songs which maintain their enduring charm and brilliance.

21: Billie Jean

Originally recorded in 1982, the song was released early in 1983, though producer, Quincy Jones, did not like it, leading to several arguments with Michael.

However, since its release, the song has become one of MJ's finest. It is a poetic narration of a woman with dementia who claims Jackson fathered one of her twin children.

The song has deep bass and a gentle enough melody you can easily play on the Kalimba with proper practice.

Tuning:

B5 G5# F5 D5 B4 G4# F4 D4 C4 E4 F4# A4 C5# E5 F5# A5

C6#

She was more like a beauty queen from a movie scene

2' 2' 2' 1' 7 1' 7 2' 7 7 1' 7 2'

I said don't mind, but what do you mean, I am the one

2' 2' 2' 2' 1' 7 1' 7 2' 1' 7 6 5

Who will dance on the floor in the round?

5 6 5 5 6 5 5 6 5

She said I am the one, who will dance on the floor in the
round

5 7 1′ 7 6 5 7 6 5 7 6 5 7 6 5

She told me her name was Billie Jean, as she caused a scene

2′ 2′ 2′ 1′ 7 1′ 7 2′ 7 7 1′ 7 2′

Then every head turned with eyes that dreamed of being the
one

2′ 2′ 2′ 2′ 1′ 7 1′ 7 2′ 1′ 1′ 7 6 5

Who will dance on the floor in the round

5 6 5 5 6 5 5 6 5

People always told me be careful of what you do

6′ 4′ 6′ 4′ 6′ 1″ 6′ 1″ 6′ 6′ 4′ 6′

And don't go around breaking young girls' hearts

2′ 6′ 4′ 6′ 6′ 6′ 4′ 6′ 7′ 6′

And mother always told me be careful of who you love

4′ 6′ 4′ 6′ 4′ 6′ 6′ 6′ 6′ 1″ 6′ 6′ 4′ 6′

And be careful of what you do 'cause the lie becomes the
truth

2′ 6′ 3′ 3′ 3′ 3′ 4′ 6′ 6′ 5′ 5′ 5′ 5′ 6′ 7′ 6′ 7′

Billie Jean is not my lover

6′ 6′ 4′ 2′ 2′ 6′ 6′ 4′ 2′

She's just a girl who claims that I am the one

6′ 6′ 6′ 4′ 2′ 2′ 6′ 1″ 2″ 1″ 7′ 6′

But the kid is not my son

6′ 6′ 3″ 2″ 2″ 6′ 3′ 2′

She says I am the one, but the kid is not my son

6′ 1″ 2″ 1″ 7′ 6′ 6′ 6′ 3″ 2″ 2″ 6′ 3′ 2′

For forty days and forty nights, the law was on her side

2′ 2′ 2′ 1′ 7 1′ 7 2′ 7 7 1′ 7 2′

But who can stand when she's in demand, her schemes and plans

2′ 2′ 2′ 2′ 1′ 7 1′ 7 2′ 1′ 7 6 5

'Cause we danced on the floor in the round

5 6 5 5 6 5 5 6 5

So take my strong advice, just remember to always think twice

5 7 1′ 7 6 5 7 6 5 7 6 5 7 6 5

She told my baby we'd danced 'til three, then she looked at me

2′ 2′ 2′ 1′ 7 1′ 7 2′ 7 7 1′ 7 2′

Then showed a photo my baby cried his eyes were like mine (oh, no)

2′ 2′ 2′ 2′ 1′ 7 1′ 7 2′ 1′ 7 6 5

'Cause we danced on the floor in the round, baby

5 6 5 5 6 5 5 6 5

People always told me be careful of what you do

6′ 4′ 6′ 4′ 6′ 1″ 6′ 1″ 6′ 6′ 4′ 6′

And don't go around breaking young girls' hearts

2′ 6′ 4′ 6′ 6′ 6′ 4′ 6′ 7′ 6′

She came and stood right by me, just the smell of sweet perfume

4′ 6′ 4′ 6′ 4′ 6′ 6′ 6′ 6′ 1″ 6′ 6′ 4′ 6′

This happened much too soon, she called me to her room

2′ 6′ 3′ 3′ 3′ 3′ 4′ 6′ 6′ 5′ 5′ 5′ 5′ 6′ 7′ 6′ 7′

Billie Jean is not my lover

6′ 6′ 4′ 2′ 2′ 6′ 6′ 4′ 2′

She's just a girl who claims that I am the one

6′ 6′ 6′ 4′ 2′ 2′ 6′ 1″ 2″ 1″ 7′ 6′

But the kid is not my son

6′ 6′ 3″ 2″ 2″ 6′ 3′ 2′

Billie Jean is not my lover

6′ 6′ 4′ 2′ 2′ 6′ 6′ 4′ 2′

She's just a girl who claims that I am the one

6′ 6′ 6′ 4′ 2′ 2′ 6′ 1″ 2″ 1″ 7′ 6′

But the kid is not my son

6′ 6′ 3″ 2″ 2″ 6′ 3′ 2′

She says I am the one, but the kid is not my son

6′ 1″ 2″ 1″ 7′ 6′ 6′ 6′ 3″ 2″ 2″ 6′ 3′ 2′

22: *Beat It*

Another smash hit from The *Thriller* album was Beat It, which MJ released a month after Billie Jean.

The song peaked at number 1 in the US Billboard Hot 100 and stayed there for three weeks. The song cemented its place as a classic as it swept all major awards at the Grammy's in 1984, including Record of the Year.

The song is RnB but fused with some Rock, which explains the strong guitar strums in the background.

However, you can still play on the Kalimba as its note is very straightforward.

Numbered Notation:

2 4 6 4° 2°

3° 2° 1° 1°

2 4 6 4° 2°

3° 2° 1°

2 4 6 4° 2°

3° 2° 1° 1°

2 4 6 4° 2°

3° 2° 1°

6° 6° 6° 5° 6° 5° 6° 1°° 6° 5° 6°

6° 6° 6° 6° 6° 6° 6° 5° 4° 5° 4° 6°

6° 5° 4° 2° 1° 2°

2° 2° 3° 2° 1° 1° 1° 2°

4° 2°

2° 3° 1°

6° 6° 6° 6° 6° 5° 6° 1°° 6° 5° 6°

6° 6° 6° 6° 6° 5° 6° 5° 4° 5° 4° 6°

6° 5° 4° 2° 2°

2° 2° 3° 2° 1°

1° 2° 4° 2°

6° 6° 1°° 6° 5°

6° 5° 6° 6°

6° 6°

6° 6° 6° 6° 1°°

6° 1°° 6°

5° 4° 5°

4° 5° 4° 5°

4° 5° 4°

5° 4° 5°

4° 5° 5°

4° 5° 4° 5° 4° 2°

2° 3° 1°

5° 4° 2°

2° 3° 1°

Lettered Notation:

D F A F° D°

E° D° C° C°

D F A F° D°

E° D° C°

D F A F° D°

E° D° C° C°

D F A F° D°

E° D° C°

A° A° A° G° A° G° A° C°° A° G° A°

A° A° A° A° A° A° A° G° F° G° F° A°

A° G° F° D° C° D°

D° D° E° D° C° C° C° D°

F° D°

D° E° C°

A° A° A° A° A° G° A° C°° A° G° A°

A° A° A° A° A° G° A° G° F° G° F° A°

A° G° F° D° D°

D° D° E° D° C°

C° D° F° D°

A° A° C°° A° G°

A° G° A° A°

A° A°

A° A° A° A° C°°

A° C°° A°

G° F° G°

F° G° F° G°

F° G° F°

G° F° G°

F° G° G°

F° G° F° G° F° D°

D° E° C°

G° F° D°

D° E° C°

23: *Smooth Criminal*

Smooth Criminal was released in 1988 from Jackson's seventh studio album, *Bad*.

The song is a pop and RnB tune, and though it did not achieve extreme success after its release, it has grown in popularity over the years. Indeed, the song's legendary status was cemented when, in the video, Michael and his dancers perform an 'anti-gravity lean.'

The song speaks of a woman who has been attacked in her apartment, with Jackson as the narrator, telling her that a 'Smooth Criminal had attacked her.'

Tabs:

6 6 3 6 7 7

6 7 1° 1°

7 1° 7 5 6

Repeat 4x

6° 6° 6° 6° 3° 6° 7° 7°

6° 7° 1° 1°

7° 1° 7° 5° 6°

Repeat 4x

6° 6° 3° 2° 6°

6° 6° 6° 6° 3° 2° 6°

6° 6° 7° 5° 6°

Repeat 2x

The Beatles

The Beatles were, at one point, the world's most well-known band. Under lead singer Paul McCartney and guitarist John Lennon, The Beatles took the world by storm, topping charts across several continents and gaining a fanatical following.

For this reason, we look at some of their classics you can play on the Kalimba.

24: Hey Jude

One of their most successful songs was Hey Jude. The single was released in August 1968 and soon hit number one in several countries around the world, including the UK, the US, Australia, and Canada.

The song is included in many lists as one of the greatest songs of all time and has sold approximately eight million copies. The song held a nine-week run at the number one Billboard Hot 100, becoming only the second song to do that.

On the Kalimba, the song is a little more complex. But with enough practice, you should get it right.

Number notes

5^0 (3^0 5) 1 3 5 1^0

3^0 5^0 6^0 2^0 2 5 7 2^0

2^0 3^0 4^0 4 1^{00} 6 1^0

1^{00} 7^0 5^0 (1 6^0) 5^0 4^0 3^0 5 1^0

5^0 (4 6^0) 6 6^0 (2^{00} 5) 1^{00}

7^0 1^{00} 6^0 5^0 1 3 5

1^0 2^0 3^0 6^0 5 5^0 7

5^0 4^0 3^0 7 1^0 1 1^0 3 5 1^0

5^0 (3^0 5) 1 3 5 1^0

3^0 5^0 6^0 2^0 2 5 7 2^0

2^0 3^0 4^0 4 1^{00} 6

1^0 1^{00} 7^0 5^0 (1 6^0) 5^0 4^0 3^0 5 1^0

5^0 (4 6^0) 6 6^0 (2^{00} 5) 1^{00}

7^0 1^{00} 6^0 5^0 1 3 5

1^0 2^0 3^0 6^0 5 5^0 7

$1\ 1^0\ 3\ 5\ 1^0$

$1\ 1^0\ 1^{00}\ 6^0\ 5^0\ 5\ 5^0\ 5^0\ 4^0\ 6^0\ 4\ 6$

$1^{00}\ 6^0\ 3\ 5\ 1^{00}\ 4^0\ 2\ 4$

$1^{00}\ 6^0\ 5\ 5^0\ 5^0\ 6^0$

$6^0\ 5^0\ 7\ 4^0\ (3^0\ 1)\ 2^0\ 1^0$

$1\ 1^0\ 1^{00}\ 6^0\ 5^0\ 5\ 5^0\ 5^0\ 4^0\ 6^0\ 4\ 6$

$1^{00}\ 6^0\ 3\ 5\ 1^{00}\ 4^0\ 2\ 4$

$1^{00}\ 6^0\ 6\ 5^0\ 4^0\ 5^0\ 2\ 5$

$6^0\ 5^0\ 7\ 4^0\ 3^0\ 1\ 2^0\ 1^0$

$1^0\ (3^0\ 3)\ 4^0\ 5^0\ 1\ 3\ 5\ 1^0$

$3^0\ 5^0\ 6^0\ 2^0\ 2\ 5\ 7\ 2^0$

$2^0\ 3^0\ 4^0\ 4\ 1^{00}\ 6\ 1^0$

$1^{00}\ 7^0\ 5^0\ (1\ 6^0)\ 5^0\ 4^0\ 3^0\ 5\ 1^0$

$5^0\ (4\ 6^0)\ 6\ 6^0\ (2^{00}\ 5\ )\ 1^{00}$

$7^0\ 1^{00}\ 6^0\ 5^0\ 1\ 3\ 5$

$1^0\ 2^0\ 3^0\ 6^0\ 5\ 5^0\ 7$

5° 4° 3° 7 1° 1 1° 3° 5° 7°

Letter notes

G^o (E^o G) C E G C^o

E^o G^o A^o D^o D G B D^o

D^o E^o F^o F C^{oo} A C^o

C^{oo} B^o G^o (C A^o) G^o F^o E^o G C^o

G^o (F A^o) A A^o (D^{oo} G) C^{oo}

B^o C^{oo} A^o G^o C E G

C^o D^o E^o A^o G G^o B

G^o F^o E^o B C^o C C^o E G C^o

G^o (E^o G) C E G C^o

E^o G^o A^o D^o D G B D^o

D^o E^o F^o F C^{oo} A

C^o C^{oo} B^o G^o (C A^o) G^o F^o E^o G C^o

G^o (F A^o) A A^o (D^{oo} G) C^{oo}

B^o C^{oo} A^o G^o C E G

D° E° A° G G° B

G° F° E° B C° C C° E G C°

C C° C°° A° G° G G° G° F° A° F A

C°° A° E G C°° F° D F

C°° A° G G° G° A°

A° G° B F° (E° C) D° C°

C C° C°° A° G° G G° G° F° A° F A

C°° A° E G C°° F° D F

C°° A° A G° F° G° D G

A° G° B F° E° C D° C°

C° (E° E) F° G° C E G C°

E° G° A° D° D G B D°

D° E° F° F C°° A C°

C°° B° G° (C A°) G° F° E° G C°

G° (F A°) A A° (D°° G) C°°

B° C°° A° G° C E G

^{o} D^o E^o A^o G G^o B

G^o F^o E^o B C^o C C^o E^o G^o B^o

25: Yesterday

Another Beatles classic is Yesterday, released in August 1965 and was part of the album *Help!*

John Lennon and Paul McCartney wrote the song. It has a smooth acoustic guitar along with a string quartet – two violinists, a cellist, and one viola player. The instruments help enhance the song's melancholic feeling, which speaks of a breakup.

The narrator, represented by Paul MacCartney, laments for the past (Yesterday) when he and his lover were still a couple before she left over something he said.

The song has been covered over 2000 times and is considered one of the most covered songs in recorded music history.

On the Kalimba, you can recreate the acoustic guitar strums with enough practice.

444

Yesterday

671°2°3°4°3°2°2°

All my troubles seemed so far away

2°2°1°765766

Now it looks as though they're here to stay

54652466

Oh, I believe in yesterday

544

Suddenly

F F

671°2°3°4°3°2°2°

Love was such an easy game to play

2°2°1°765766

Now I need a place to hide away

54652466

Oh, I believe in yesterday

662°3°4°3°2°3°2°1°2°6

Why she had to go, I don't know, she wouldn't say

662°3°4°3°2°3°2°1°3°4°1°76

I said something wrong, now I long for yesterday

544

Yesterday

671°2°3°4°3°2°2°

Love was such an easy game to play

2°2°1°765766

Now I need a place to hide away

54652466

Oh, I believe in yesterday

4652466

Mm mm mm mm mm mm mm

26: I Will

'I Will' was from the 1968 album called *The Beatles,* later known as 'The White Album.'

The track was a love ballad and speaks of a man who declares his undying love for a woman whose name he still doesn't know. Thus, he declares, 'I will always feel the same,' meaning he will always love the woman.

On the Kalimba, the song is quite easy to play.

7 1° 5° 3° 1° 2° 4°

7 1° 5° 3° 1° 5°

5° 1° ° 4° 2° 5° 3° 1°

5° 1° 6° 4° 2° 1° 1°

7 1° 5° 3° 1° 2° 4°

7 1° 5° 3° 1° 5°

5° 1° ° 4° 2° 5° 3° 1°

5° 1° 6° 4° 2° 1° 1°

2° 4° 3° 4° 5° 6° 3° 1° 2° 3°

2° 4° 3° 4° 5° 6° 3°

2° 4° 3° 4° 5° 6° 3° 1° 2° 3°

2° 4° 3° 4° 4° 5° 5°

7 1° 5° 3° 1° 2° 4°

7 1° 5° 3° 1° 5°

5° 1° ° 4° 2° 5° 3° 1°

5° 1° ° 4° 2° 5° 3° 1°

5° 1° 6° 4° 2° 5° 1° 6° 5° 1°

6° 4° 2° 1° 1°

6° 4° 2° 1° 1°

°1 °2 °3 °4 °5

27: *In My Life*

In My Life was released in 1956 as part of the classic album *Rubber Soul* and was written by John Lennon and Paul McCartney.

The song was a meditation piece for John Lennon, where he reflected on his past, with Paul McCartney working with him to refine the lyrics.

The song is among those considered the 100 greatest songs of all time and has also been extensively covered.

The song features a strong rhythm guitar that gives the song its distinctive melody. On the Kalimba, you will have to play quite a handful of chords. However, with time, you should be able to muster it.

(31) 31" 4' 5' (75) (31) 31" 4' 5' (7'5)

56 (21) 3 1'5 (21) 33' 5 (5'1) 3' 357

23 (21) 35 35 (51) 3'

5 (61) 33' (31)

56 (21) 3 1'5 (21) 33'5 (51) 3' 357

2'3 (21) 353'2' 1'13

5 (61) 33 (31)

1'2' (31) 3216 (31) 2 357

3' (41) 3' 2'1135

5 (61) 3 3' (31)

1'2' (31) 32' 1'6 (31) 2 357

2 (31) 2'1135

5 (61) 33' (3'1)

(31) 31" 3' 45' (75)

56 (21) 3 1'5' (21) 33' 5 (51)

357

2'3 (21) 353'2' 1'13

5 (61) 33 (31)

56 (21) 3 1'5'(21) 33' 5 (51) 3'

357

2'3 (21) 353' 21'13

5 (61) 33' (31)|

1'2' (31) 32'1' 61' 2' (3'1) 2' 357

3' (41) 3'2' 1'135

5 (61) 3 3' (3'1) 357

2' (3'1) 2' 1' 61' 61'2' (3'1) 2'

357

2' (3'1) 2' 1' 2' 1'13

2 (61) 3 3' (3'1)

(31) 31" 3' 4' 5' (7'5)

(7'5) 6' 7' (1'1)|

28: Ode to Joy - Beethoven

Another from Ludwig van Beethoven is Ode to Joy, the Symphony No 9 of the legendary classical music composer.

Beethoven first performed this song in Vienna in 1824. The song is about peace, with the Ode to Joy representing the joy of the triumph of universal unity and brotherhood over war.

We can describe the song's nature as joyful and dramatic, though you will need proper practice to play the chords, most of which are made up of notes on opposite sides of the Kalimba.

Letter notes

EEFG GFED

CCDEE DD

EEFG GFED

CCDED CC

DDEC DEFEC

D EFE DC DD

EEFG GFED

CCDED CC

Number notation

3345 543$2$

11233 22

3345 543$2$

11232 11

2231 23431

2 343 21 22

3345 543$2$

11232 11

29: *Air on the G String – J S Bach*

This classical song was rearranged by August Wilhelmj, who changed the original key from D major to a C major. Thus, you can play the rearranged version much easier on the Kalimba, which comes tuned to the C major key.

Wilhelmj made this arrangement in 1871, and this version became popular among many people who have transferred the piece onto other musical pieces.

While not as straightforward as the other songs on this list, enough practice should help you manage to play the piece without too many hiccups.

(4 4' 6') 4' 3' 3 (24' 6') 2' 1'1

7 (2' 2'') 7' (3 5') 4' 3' 4' (1 3') 1' 2' 1'1

(6 1'') 3'1' 32 6' 6 2' (7 5') 1' 1'' 7'

(57) 2'7435' (7 2') 1' 4' 3' (17) 6'

(46) 4' 3'31'' (24) 4' 5' 6' (6 6') 5' (7 5') 4' (53) 2'2' 3' 4' (1' 4')
3' 2' (1 1) 2345765 (1 3') 1' 74' 3'2' 3' 1' (6 1'') 3' 6 (3 3')

(22) (7 2'') 1' 1'' (2' 7') 6' (57) 7 5 6' 5' 4' 3' 2' 12'3'34' (75) 6 6'
(2' 7') 1' 6'

(5 5') 4' 3' 2' (73) 4' 5' 4' 3 (22) 2' 1'1

(3 1') 3' 53' (7 5') 7' (4' 7') 5' 6' 4' (1'6') 7' 1'' (24) 2' 1'6' (1 1'')
3'' (7 2'') 7' 6' (64')

(7 3') 5' (57) 32' (1 1') (3 5') 6' 7' (4' 7') 6' 7 5'

(64') 3' 2' 53' (1' 4') (1 2) 3' (4 6 1'4')

30: The Animals – The House of the Rising Sun

The House of the Rising Sun was a traditional British folk song that spoke of a woman's life going wrong after she moved to New Orleans. The song, then, urges the person's sibling, parent, and children to avoid the same fate.

However, when the rock band The Animals covered it in 1964, it became well known and received. The Animals' cover song sang about a New Orleans brothel, and the song was an instant hit.

The song topped the UK Singles Charts, the US, Canada, and has gained the distinction of being the first folk-rock hit song.

To play it on the Kalimba, you will have to play a lot of half notes and chords; thus, it will need a fair bit of practice before you get it right.

Tabs:

(136) 1° 3°

1° (1°1) (1°35) 3°

1° 2 6 2°

6 4 6 1°

7 (63) 1° 3°

1° 3 7 3°

7 (63) 1° 3°

1° 3 7 3°

5 (136) 3 6

7 (1°1) (35) 1°

3° (22°) 6 6

2° 4 (61°) 4°

6° (136°) (361°) 3°

6° (15°) (351°) 3°

2° (33°) 7 3°

7 3 7 3° 6° 6° (136°)

3 6 7 (11°) 1°

3 5 3° (22°)

6 6 5 (46)

1° 4° 5 (136)

3 6 1° (37)

3 7 1° (136)

1° 3° 1° (1°1)

(351°) 3° 1° 2

6 2° 6 4

61° 7 (36)

1° 3° 1° 3

7 3° 7 (36)

1° 3° 1° 3 7 3° 7 6° 6° (136°)

(361°) 3° 6° (15°)

3° 5 1° (22°)

6 6 5 (46)

1° 4° 6° 6° (136°)

(361°) 3° 6° (15°)

(1°35) 3° 2° (33°)

7 3° 7 3

7 3° 6° 6° (136°)

3 6 7 (11°) 1° (13) 5

3° (22°) 6 6

5 (46) 1° 4°

5 (136) 3 6

1° (37) 3 7

1° (136) 1° 3° 1

(361°) 3° 2 6 2° 4

6 1° (136) 1° 3°

3 7 3°

(136) 1° 3° 3 7 3° (33°)

31: *Away in a Manger*

Away in a Manger is a Christmas carol first published around the late 19th century.

The song details the moment after Jesus had been born, with his parents and all the animals in the shed in awe of the newly born savior.

The song is thought to have been the work of German music composer Martin Luther. However, recent history suggests it could be wholly American in origin.

The current melody and musical setting was the work of William J Kirkpatrick (1895) and James Ramsey Murray (1887), both of whom were American hymn writers and musical composers.

The song is a timeless and slow Christmas carol which you can easily transfer to the Kalimba. The song makes good use of chords; thus, you will need a little bit of practice before getting it right.

Numbered Notation:

5° (1°3°5°)

4° 3° (3°1°) 2° 1° (61°) (57) 6 (135)

5 5

6 5 5 2° 7 6 5 1° (1°3°) 5 1° 2° 3° 4° (1°3°5°)

4° (1°3°) (1°3°) (72°) 1° (61°) (57) (46) (135)

5 (572°4°)

3° 2° (1°3°) (72°) (61°) (62°) 6 (57)

(1° 135)

Lettered Notation:

G° (C°E°G°)

F° E° (E°C°) D° C° (AC°) (GB) A (CEG)

G G

A G G D° B A G C° (C°E°) G C° D° E° F° (C°E°G°)

F° (C°E°) (C°E°) (BD°) C° (AC°) (GB) (FA) (CEG)

G (GBD°F°)

E° D° (C°E°) (BD°) (AC°) (AD°) A (GB)

(C° CEG)

•

32: All I Have to Do Is Dream –Everly Brothers

Though the Everly Brothers performed this song, they weren't the original composers of the music. Songwriting couple Felice and Boudleaux Bryant were the original songwriters.

The Everly Brothers released it in April 1958, and while the song did not peak very high in charts, it soon grew a following as time went on. Now, it is considered as part of the 500 Greatest Songs of All Time.

The song was even featured recently in the 2010 Nightmare on Elm Street movie remake.

The track's slow tempo makes it rather easy for you to play on the Kalimba.

1/3° 2° 1° 5 6

4/6° 6° 5/5° 4°

1/3° 2° 1° 5 6

4/6° 6° 5/5° 4°

1/3° 3° 6/3°

4 /4° 4° 5/5° 4°

1/3° 3° 6/3°

4/4° 4° 4° 5/5° 4°

1/3° 2° 3° 6/6° 3° 2°|

4/1° 1° 1° 1° 5/2° 2°

1/3° 2° 1° 5 6

4/6° 6° 5/5° 4°

1/3° 3° 6/3°

4 /4° 4° 5/5° 4°

1/3° 3° 2° 6/3°

4/4° 4° 4° 5/5° 4°

1/3° 2° 3° 6/6° 3° 2°

4/1° 1° 1° 1° 5/2° 2°

1/3° 2° 1° 4

1 1

4/6° 6° 6° 6° 6°

3/5° 5° 5° 5° 5°

2/4° 4° 4° 5 /5° 4°

1/3°

4/6° 6° 6° 6° 6°

3 /7° 6° 5° 5°

2/6° 6° 6° 6°/5° 4°

5/5° 4°

1/3° 3° 6/3°

4/4° 4° 4° 5/5° 4°

1/3° 3° 6/3°

4/4° 4° 4° 5/5° 4°

1/3° 2° 3° 6/6° 3° 2°

4/1° 1° 1° 1° 5/2° 2°

1/3° 2° 1° 5 6

4/6° 6° 5/5° 4°

1/3° 2° 1° 4

1 1

4/6° 6° 6° 6° 6°

3/5° 5° 5° 5° 5°

2/4° 4° 4° 5 /5° 4°

1/3°

4/6° 6° 6° 6° 6°

3 /7° 6° 5° 5°

2/6° 6° 6° 6°/5° 4°

5/5° 4°

1/3° 3° 6/3°

4/4° 4° 4° 5/5° 4°

1/3° 3° 6/3°

4/4° 4° 4° 5/5° 4°

1/3° 2° 3° 6/6° 3° 2°

4/1° 1° 1° 1° 5/2° 2°

1/3° 2° 1° 5 6

4/6° 6° 5/5° 4°

1/3° 2° 1° 5 6

4/6° 6° 5/5° 4°

1/3° 2° 1° 5 6

4/6° 6° 5/5° 4°

1/3° 2° 1°

The Rolling Stones

The Rolling Stones is an English Band that has been active since 1962, with most of their most iconic songs coming during the 60s, where they got to define the hard rock genre of music.

The band's music style means that recreating it on the Kalimba can be quite challenging but still doable. Below, we look at some of their songs you can play on the Kalimba.

33: Paint it Black

This song was recorded in 1966 and released that same year. However, upon its releases, the song was panned by critics for what they believed was The Rolling Stones attempting to copy The Beatles.

However, the song still went on to be a classic and is ranked as one of the Greatest Songs of all time in several lists.

The song has an upbeat tempo even though it speaks of grief and loss. It also draws influence from Middle Eastern and Eastern Europe and features an Indian sitar (a type of Indian plucked stringed instrument that looks like a stretched-out ukulele).

Tuning:

C tone: A = Ab, B=Bb, D5=C5#

Intro:

4 5 6 (357) 6 5 4 4 3 4 5 2̇345 4̇32̇3

Verse 1:

(124) 5 6 7 6 5 4 (124) 3 4 5 4 3 (x2 times)

(4̇4) 2′ 2′ (246) 6 7 7 (1̇1) (1̇3) 7 6 (1̇5) (x 2 times)

Repeat Verse 1

Verse 2:

(41) 5 6 (72) 6 5 4 (41) 3 4 5 (41) 3 (x2 times)

(4̇4) 2′ 2′ (246) 6 7 7 (1̇1) (1̇3) 7 6 (1̇5) (x 2 times)

(1̇1) 1′ 3′ 3′ 3′ 3′ 3′ 3′ (4̇4)

(4̇4) 4′|4′ (3̇3) 1′ 1′

1′ (4̇4) 3′ 4′ 3′ 4′

(4̇4) 4′ 2′ (1̇1) 1′ 1′

3′ (4̇4) 3′ 4′ 3′ (4̇4) 1′

(4̇4) 1′ (4̇4) 1′ (4̇4) 4′ 3′ (4̇4)

34: *Ruby Tuesday*

Ruby Tuesday is another of The Rolling Stones' classics. Released in 1966, the song was The Rolling Stones' fourth song to hit number one in the United States.

Its popularity saw it covered yearly from its release until 1970. The covers would soon resume in 1989, and others in 1993 and 1994.

Keith Richards, the band's guitarist, wrote this song after his girlfriend left him for another famous rock star. The track features strong guitar riffs and a flute, which means it would sound great on the Kalimba.

VERSE 1

6651°4

She would never say

1235

where she came from

6651°44

Yesterday don't matter

235

if it's gone

661°1°5

While the sun is bright

5661°1°5

Or in the darkest night

243

No one knows,

1235

she comes and goes

CHORUS

$3° \ 2° \ 4° \ 3°2°1°$

Goodbye Ruby Tuesday

$3° \ 3°2°2°2°3°2°$

Who could hang a name on you?

3° 3°2°2°1°1°1°1°

When you change with every new day

2°2°2°3°4°3°

Still I'm gonna miss you

VERSE 2

56651°4

Don't question why she needs

1235

to be so free

6651°44

She'll tell you it's the only

♮235

way to be

661°1°5

She just can't be chained

5661°1°5

To a life where nothing's gained

243

Or nothing's lost,

1235

at such a cost

Repeat CHORUS

VERSE 3 = VERSE 1

Repeat CHORUS

Repeat CHORUS

35: Angie

Angie was the lead single of one of The Rolling Stones' most successful albums, *Goats Head Soup.*

Released in 1973, the song is a heartbreak song that features strong acoustic guitars and a distinctive piano accompaniment. It peaked at number one soon after its release in the US Billboard Hot 100 while also topping charts in Canada and Australia.

The song is major on chords and will need proper practice to get right.

Letter Notation:

(E'C'A)E' E'

(E'G'B') E'D'

(GBD') D' D' D'D (FAC'D') C'AD' (C'E'

G') E'D' C'

(A C'E') E' E'

(E'G'B') E' D'

(EG BD') E' E' D' (FAC' D') C' A D' (C'E' G')

E' D'C'

E' E' (GBD' E') D' D' E' (GBD') D' D' (DFA D') D' D'C' (AC'E')

(AC'E')|

E' G'A'G' G'

E' (G' GBD') E' D'

(GBD')

(AC'E')

E'

E'

(E'G'B') E'

D'

(GBD')

D' D' (FAC' D') C'C' A D' (C'E'G') E'D'

(AC'E') E' E'

C' (E'G'B') E' D'

(GBD') D' D'D' (FAC' D') C'C' A (C'E' G'D')

E' D' C'

(AC'E') E'

E'

(E'G'B') E' E' D' E'

(GBD') D' D'D' (FAC'E') D' C' A D' (C'E'G') E'

D' C'

E' E' (E' GB D') D' D'E' (GBD')

D' C' (DFA D') D' D' C

(AC'E')

(ACE)

E' O' (FAC' A') G'G'E (G OBD')G' E' D'

(GBD')

(AC'E') E

(E'G'B') E'

(GBD') D' D' D' (FAC' D') CAD (C'E'G') E' D'C'

AE (AC) BBA (EA) A

EBB'A' A'E (GB) E

FC (BF) A G'A (CD) (GF) A' (C'A') G|C

AE (AC) B C (AA) E' A'

EBBA'B' (GE) (EB) E'

FB'B' (BF) A' G'GA (G'D') A' GCFG (CF) (GE) CEC'O' C

(EG) D' (EG) D' D'ED' (G'D')

(DD) (CA) D' D' (AD') C'E' (AA)

A (C'E') (E'A') & (AA) (E'G') (G'A') E (GG) E' D'G'

G' D'G'D' (AC'E') E

(E'G'B') D'

36: Here Comes Santa – Gene Autry

Once again, we have another Christmas classic on this list. Here Comes Santa was performed by Gene Autry in 1947.

Autry combines the Christmas traditions of the Santa Clause mythologies and the origins of Christmas for this catchy country music.

The song peaked at number 5 in the 1948 US Billboard Hot Country singles, and it remains a high-performing song in the charts, often found among the top 30 in the US and Global Billboards.

The song makes great use of chords, especially at the beginning of a new line. It prominently features a saxophone and flute and has great use of the keyboard percussion. Throughout the song, there is also a constant jingle of Christmas bells. Thus, with enough practice, you should be able to play it well.

Numbered Notation:

(15) 3° 2° 2° 1°

(15) 3° 2° 2° 1°

(25) 4° 4° 4° 3° (24°)

(25) 4° 4° 3° 2°

5 5 4° 3° 4°

(15°) 5° 5° 6° 5° 1 3

(46°) 1°° 7° 6°

(35°) 7° 6° 5°

(24°) 4° 6° 5° 4° (13°) 3

5° (46°) 1°° 7° 6°

6° (35°) 7° 6° 5°

3° (25°) 5° 4° (53°) 2° 1° 1 3

(15) 3° 2° 2° 1°

(15) 3° 2° 2° 1°

(25) 4° 4° 4° 3° (24°)

(25) 4° 4° 3° 2°

5 5 4° 3° 4°

(15°) 5° 5° 6° 5° 1 3

(46°) 1°° 7° 6°

(35°) 7° 6° 5°

(24°) 4° 6° 5° 4° (13°) 3

5 (46°) 1°° 7° 6°

6° (35°) 7° 6° 5°

3° (25°) 5° 4° (53°) 2° 1° (135)

Lettered Notation:

(CG) E° D° D° C°

(CG) E° D° D° C°

(DG) F° F° F° E° (DF°)

(DG) F° F° E° D°

G G F° E° F°

(CG°) G° G° A° G° C E

(FA°) C°° B° A°

(EG°) B° A° G°

(DF°) F° A° G° F° (CE°) E

G° (FA°) C°° B° A°

A° (EG°) B° A° G°
E° (DG°) G° F° (GE°) D° C° C E

(CG) E° D° D° C°
(CG) E° D° D° C°
(DG) F° F° F° E° (DF°)
(DG) F° F° E° D°
G G F° E° F°
(CG°) G° G° A° G° C E
(FA°) C°° B° A°
(EG°) B° A° G°
(DF°) F° A° G° F° (CE°) E
G (FA°) C°° B° A°
A° (EG°) B° A° G°
E° (DG°) G° F° (GE°) D° C° (CEG)

37: Beauty and The Beast

Yet another song from a movie that went on to be a classic, Beauty and the Beast (1991), was recorded for the movie of the same name.

The song calls on us to show kindness to others beyond the outward appearance, which is signified when the beauty falls in love with the beast due to his kindness, overlooking his beastly outward looks.

The song has been covered in the remakes of the movie, but the original has managed to create a lasting legacy, becoming a classic in its own right.

Tale as old as time

(1 3) 1 3 5 7 1' 4-1 1 2 3 4 2 (1 3) 1

True as it can be

3 5 7 1' (5 7 2')-2 5 2' 4' 3-(1 3 5) 1

Barely even friends

1' 2' 3' 4' 5'-3 5 7 1'

then somebody bends

5' 4' 3' 2' (4 6 1')-1 1 4 6

unexpectedly

4' 3' 2' 1' 5-2 2 5 5-2 4 (1 3) 1

Just a little change

3 5 7 1' 4-1 1 2 3 4 2 (1 3) 1

Small, to say the least

3 5 7 1' (5 7 2')-2 5

Both a little scared

3'-1 2' 3'-3 5' (4 6 1)-1 1 4 6

neither one prepared

(4 6 1')-1 7 1'-3 3' (2 4) 2 4 6

Beauty and the Beast

3'-5 4' 2' 3' 1'-(1 3 5) 2 3 5 1' 2' 3' 5' 1" 1

38: Singin' in the Rain – Gene Kelly

Singin' in the rain was the theme song for a movie of the same name released in 1952. Gene Kelly, the main actor in the movie, sang the song in the musical. Both the song and the movie would go on to become classics in their own rights.

Arthur Freed, a prominent songwriter, wrote the song, with Nacio Herb Brown as the composer.

Since then, the song has been covered extensively, even re-entering the top charts in 2008, when it peaked at no. 1 in the UK Singles Chart after a rendition performance on *Britain's Got Talent* show.

The song has an upbeat tempo and features strong violin sounds in the background.

Numbered Notation:

2 2° 7 6 5 3

2 5 5 6 7 2

2 3 5 6 7 2

7 2° 2° 7 6 3

2 2° 7 6 3

2 2° 7 6 3

2 2° 7 3 4 7 3 5

3 5 3

2 3 5 6 7 2°

2 3 5 6 7 2°

2 5 6 7 2°

7 2° 2° 7 6 3

2 2° 7 6 3

2° 1° 2° 7 6 3

2 2° 2° 2 4 4 2° 2 5

Lettered Notation:

D D° B A G E

D G G A B D

D E G A B D

B D° D° B A E

D D° B A E

D D° B A E

D D° B E F B E G

E G E

D E G A B D°

D E G A B D°

D G A B D°

B D° D° B A E

D D° B A E

D° C° D° B A E

D D° D° D F F D° D G

The Carpenters

The Carpenters were a singing duet that featured siblings Karen and Richard Carpenter. The two produced a distinctly soft style of music, even though they occasionally sang some rock music.

Below are some of their classic songs you can play on the Kalimba.

39: *I Won't Last a Day Without You*

Released in 1974, the track was a hit single, reaching No 11 in the Billboard Hot 100 charts. It was the 14th single from the siblings to hit the Billboard top 100.

The song is a slow love ballad that sounds even more heavenly when paired with Karen's smooth harmonization.

It is no doubt a song you will enjoy playing on the Kalimba.

G G–A G G G G F F E E – D

Day after day I must face a world of strangers

C D E B – B E F C° C°

Where I don't belong, I'm not that strong

G G A G G G G – F F E E D

It's nice to know that there's someone I can turn to

C D E – B B E F – C° C°

Who will always care, you're always there...

C° D° E° E°-E° E°-D° E° C°-A-C^

When there's no getting over that rainbow

C° D° E°-E° E° E° D° E° C°

When my smallest of dreams won't come true

E° F° G° G° G° G° – F° G° E° C° A C°

I can take all the madness the world has to give

A C° F° E° C° G F – G G

But I won't last a day without you!

40: Top of The World

Released in 1972, Top of The World became a hit in 1973, spending two consecutive weeks in the Billboard Hot 100 No. 1.

The song features strong electronic piano sounds, a bass guitar, and drums, with Richard Carpenter providing background for Karen's strong leading vocals.

On the Kalimba, the song prominently features half notes.

(5 7) (6 4)

(2 7) (1° 3) (2° 4)

3° 3° 3° 4° 3° 2° 1°

6 1° 1° 2 1° 7 6 5

3° 2° 1° 7 6 7 1° (1° 3° 5°)

3 3 4 2

3 3 4 2

3 3 4 2

3 1 1 1

5 3° 2° 1° 7 1° 6 7 5

3° 4° 5° 5° 5° 3° 2° 3° 4° 2° 3°

4° 5° 6° 6° 4° 2° 2° 6° 5° 4° 5° 3°

2° 3° 4° 4° 3° 4° 3° 2° 1° 5

5 3° 2° 1° 7 1° 6° 7 5°

3° 4° 5° 5° 5° 3° 2° 3° 4° 6° 5°

4° 5° 6° 6° 4° 2° 2° 6° ♭5° 4° 5° 3°

2° 3° 4° 4° 4° 3° 4° 3° 2° 1° 5°

5 1° 2° (1 3) 3° 3° 3° 4° 3° 2° 1° (6 4) 6° 6° 6° 7° 6°

5° 4° 3° 5° 3° 4° 2° 3° 4° 6° 5°

4° 5° 6° 5° 6° 7° 6° 7° 1°° 1°° 1° 5° 6°

5° 4° 3° 5° 4° 3° 2° 1° 7 1°

5 1° 2° (1 3) 3° 3° 3° 4° 3° 2° 1° (6 4) 6° 6° 6° 7° 6°

5° 4° 3° 5° 3° 4° 2° 3° 4° 6° 5°

4° 5° 6° 5° 6° 7° 6° 7° 1°° 1°° 1° 5° 6°

5° 4° 3° 5° 4° 3° 1° 7 1°

5° 4° 3° 5° 4° 3° 2° 1° 7 1°

3 3 4 2

3 3 4 2

3 3 4 2

3 (5 7) (6 1)

Chapter 4: Modern Songs to Play on the Kalimba

If you would also like to play your modern-day favorites on the Kalimba, well, you should also know that the Kalimba can play modern songs just fine.

This section looks at some of the hits from prominent artists you can recreate on your Kalimba.

41: Faded – Alan Walker

Faded is a song by Music Producer and DJ Alan Walker, with singer, Iselin Solheim, providing the vocals.

The song was released in 2015 and became a huge hit. It is now among the most viewed videos on YouTube, with over 3 billion views. On the Kalimba, here is how you will play it:

Number notes

(61° 3) 3 1° 3

1° 3 3° 3

(4 6°) 1° (66°) 1°

(46°) 1° (5°6) 1°

(3° 1) 5 (3°3) 5

(3°1) 5 (3°3) 5

(257) 2 5 2

7 2 1° 7

(63) 1° 1° 6

1° 6 1° 2°

(3°1°) 1° 1°

5 3° 3°

1 5 3 5

1 (1° 5) (1° 3) (1° 5)

(2 5 7) 2 5 1°

7 6 1°

(63) 1° 1° 6

1° 6 1° 2°

(61°3°) 1° 1°

5° 3° 3°

1 5 3 5

1 (1° 5) (1°3) (1°5)

(257) 2 5 2

7 3° 3° 3°

(61°3° 3) 3 6 3

1° 1° 1° 1°

(46 1) 5 1 5

3 1° 5° 5°

(3° 1) 5 3 5

1 (3°5) (5° 3) (5°5)

(2 572°) 2 5 2

2° 3° 3° 3°

(61°3° 3) 3 6 3

1° 1° 1° 6

(4 4°) 1° 6 1°

4 1° 5° 5°

(3°1°) 5 3 5

1 (1°5) (5°3) (5° 5)

(25°72°) 2 5 2

4° 3° 2° 1°

(63)

Letter notes

(AC° E) E C° E

C° E E° E

(FA°) C° (G°A) C°

(E° C) G (E°E) G

(E°C) G (E°E) G

(DGB) D G D

B D C° B

(AE) C° C° A

C° A C° D°

(E°C°) C° C°

G E° E°

C G E G

C (C° G) (C° E) (C° G)

(D G B) D G C°

B A C°

(AE) C° C° A

C° A C° D°

(AC°E°) C° C°

G° E° E°

C G E G

C (C° G) (C°E) (C°G)

(DGB) D G D

B E° E° E°

(AC°E° E) E A E

C° C° C° C°

(FA C) G C G

E C° G° G°

(E° C) G E G

C (E°G) (G° E) (G°G)

(D GBD°) D G D

D° E° E° E°

(AC°E° E) E A E

C° C° C° A

(F F°) C° A C°

F C° G° G°

(E°C°) G E G

C (C°G) (G°E) (G° G)

(DG°BD°) D G D

F° E° D° C°

(AE)

Ed Sheeran

As one of the most successful contemporary artists, Ed Sheeran has inspired a generation, with most of his songs receiving extensive cover across various musical instruments since his breakout around 2010.

Below are some of his most beloved songs that you can play on the Kalimba.

42: Perfect

Perfect was Ed Sheeran's most successful single off his 2017 album, Divide. The soft rock/ pop song peaked in the UK Singles Charts and the US Billboard Hot 100. It would also peak in sixteen other countries.

The love ballad is set to a slow tempo of 63 beats per minute, which recreates wonderfully on the Kalimba:

♮ 6 1° 1°

3° 2° 1° 3°

2° 3° 3° 1°

1° 2° 3° 2°

3° 2° 1° 3°

5° 3° 2° 1°

1° 2° 3° 4°

4° 3° 3° 2°

1° 2° 3° 2°

5° 5° 5°

6° 3° 2°

3° 3° 3° 3° 2° 1° 3° 3° 3°

3° 2° 1° 4° 3° 2° 1°

5 3° 4° 3° 2°

3° 2° 1° 3° 3° 3°

3° 2° 1° 3° 3° 3°

3° 2° 1° 4° 3° 2° 1°

5 3° 4° 3° 2°

3° 2° 1° 1°° 7° 6° 7° 3°

5° 4° 3° 4° 3°

1°° 7° 6° 7° 3° 5° 5° 5° 5°

6° 3° 2° 1°

3° 5° 1°° 7° 6° 7° 3°

1° 2° 3° 5°

4° 3° 4° 3°

2° 4° 3° 1° 2° 3° 2° 2° 1° 7 1°

43: *Shape of You*

Another song from the Divide Album, Shape of You, is probably Ed Sheeran's biggest song.

After its release, the song set some records, including the most-streamed song on Spotify, surpassing 2 billion streams on the music platform.

It is also the second best-selling song digitally and was named as one of the number one songs of the 2010s. The song is set at a moderately fast 96 beats per minute and has a steady rhythm.

Letter notes

A C° A A C° A A C° A B A G ×2

C° C° C° C° C° C° C° C° D° E° E°

G° D° D° D° D° D° D° D° E° D° C° A

A E° E° E° E° E° E° E° D° C° E° D° C°

G° D° D° D° D° D° D° D° E° D° C° A

E G A G A A G A E° D° D° D° C° A C° E° D° C° A

G° E° D° E° D° C° A

Number notation

6 1° 6 6 1° 6 6 1° 6 7 6 5 ×2

1° 1° 1° 1° 1° 1° 1° 1° 2° 3° 3°

5° 2° 2° 2° 2° 2° 2° 2° 3° 2° 1° 6

6 3° 3° 3° 3° 3° 3° 3° 3° 2° 1° 3° 2° 1°

5° 2° 2° 2° 2° 2° 2° 2° 3° 2° 1° 6

3 5 6 5 6 6 5 6 3° 2° 2° 2° 1° 6 1° 3° 2° 1° 6

5° 3° 2° 3° 2° 1° 6

Justin Bieber

Justine Bieber broke into the public limelight as a 16-year-old prodigy and has never looked back since then.

As one of the world's most beloved RnB and Pop artists, his songs have been extensively played on different instruments. Below, we look at his most popular songs played on the Kalimba.

44: Yummy

Yummy was released in January of 2020 to mixed reception, with many questioning the song production. Justin Bieber's vocals and delivery, and the song's lyrics, also came under scrutiny.

Despite that, the song went on to be a huge success.

Here are the notes to play Yummy on the Kalimba

$$^{-}\,444444$$

$$3333$$

$$6_1{}^\circ 1^\circ 2^\circ 6_{55}$$

$$46_5546554$$

$$6_1{}^\circ 1^\circ 2^\circ 6_{55}$$

$$46_5541^\circ 55$$

$$1^\circ 1^\circ 64^\circ 4^\circ 1^\circ$$

$$6^\circ 5^\circ 6^\circ 5^\circ 6^\circ 5^\circ$$

$$6^\circ 5^\circ 5^\circ 6^\circ 5^\circ 5^\circ$$

$$1^\circ 1^\circ 64^\circ 4^\circ 1^\circ |$$

$$6^\circ 5^\circ 6^\circ 5^\circ 6^\circ 5^\circ$$

$$6^\circ 5^\circ 5^\circ 5^\circ 1^{\circ\circ} 5^\circ 4^\circ$$

$$1^\circ 1^\circ 64^\circ 4^\circ 1^\circ$$

$$6_1{}^\circ 1^\circ 2^\circ 6_{55}$$

$$46_5546554$$

$$6_1{}^\circ 1^\circ 2^\circ 6_{55}$$

$$46_5541^\circ 55$$

$$1^\circ 1^\circ 64^\circ 4^\circ 1^\circ$$

$$6^\circ 5^\circ 6^\circ 5^\circ 6^\circ 5^\circ$$

$$6^\circ 5^\circ 6^\circ 5^\circ 6^\circ 5^\circ$$

$$1^\circ 1^\circ 64^\circ 4^\circ 1^\circ$$

$$6^\circ 5^\circ 6^\circ 5^\circ 6^\circ 5^\circ$$

$$6^\circ 5^\circ 5^\circ 5^\circ 1^{\circ\circ} 5^\circ 4^\circ$$

$$1^\circ 1^\circ 64^\circ 4^\circ 1^\circ$$

45: Let me Love You

This song is credited to DJ Snake, who produced and recorded the song, with Justin Bieber providing the vocals.

The song is an electronic pop song set to a moderately fast tempo of 100 beats per minute.

Here is how to play Let Me Love You on the Kalimba

-

66 566 566 566

544 344 344 344

3'5'3' 6' 3'5' 6' 5'5' 3'3'

2'2' 1'2'3' 61'

3'5'3' 6' 3'5' 6' 5'5' 3'3'

2'2' 1'2'3' 6'1'

2' 1'2'3' 61'

1'1' 61'1' 63'

77 577 52'

2' 2'2' 2' 2'3'4'4' 3'1' 6

1'1' 61'1' 63'

77 577 52'

2' 2'2' 2' 2'3'4'4' 3'1'

1'2'3'3' 1' 1'1'

1'2'3'3' 1' 1'1'

1'2'3'3' 7 77

4' 3'3'6 4' 3'3'1'

1'2'3'3' 1' 1'1'

1'2'3'3' 7 77

4' 3'3'6 4' 3'3'1'|

1'1' 3'2' 1'1' 3'2'

61'61' 3'6

61'64' 3'1'

1'1' 3'2' 1'1' 3'2'

61'64' 3'6

61'64' 3'1'

3'5'3' 6' 3'5' 6' 5'5' 3'3'

2'2' 1'2'3' 61'

2' 1'2'3' 61'

3'5'3' 6' 3'5' 6' 5'5' 3'3'

2'2' 1'2'3' 61'

2' 1'2'3' 61'

1'1' 61'1' 62'

77 577 52'

2' 2'2' 2' 2'3'4'4' 3'1' 6

1'1' 61'1' 63'

77 577 52'

2' 2'2' 2' 2'3'4'4' 3'1'

1'2'3'3' 1' 1'1'

1'2'3'3' 7 77

4' 3'3'6' 4' 3'3'1'

1'2'3'3' 1' 1'1'

1'2'3'3' 7 77

4' 3'3'6 4' 3'3'1'

1'1' 3'2' 1'1' 3'2'

61'64' 3'6|

61'64' 3'1'

1'1' 3'2' 1'1' 3'2'

61'64' 3'6

61'64' 3'1'

46: Love Yourself

Written by Ed Sheeran, Love Yourself was the third single from Justin Bieber's critically acclaimed album, Purpose, released in 2015.

The song details the protagonist telling off an ex-lover who wronged him, asking her to go love herself first before trying to love others.

Bieber used a low husky voice for this song which blends well with the acoustics on the background and brings out the pain and hurt in the song.

Here is how to play love Yourself on the Kalimba

- 1• 2• 3• 1 3 3• 3• (2• − 4) 2• 3• 2• (1• − 1) 3 5

For all the times that you rained on my parade

1• 2• 3• 4• 4 4• 3• 2• (1• − 1) 2• 3• 2• 2 5 7

And all the clubs you get in using my name

1• 1• 2• 3• 1 5• 2• 1• (2• − 2) 3• 2• 1• 1 1• 3

You think you broke my heart, oh girl for goodness sake

1• 2• 3• 4• 4 4• 3• 2• (1• − 1) 2• 3• 2• 2 5 7

You think I'm crying on my own, well I ain't

1• 1• 2• (3• − 1) 5• 3• 3

And I didn't wanna write a song

5• 5• 4• (4• − 4) 3• 2• 1• 1• 2• 3•

'cause I didn't want anyone thinking I still care

1• (2• − 2) 3• 1• 2• 3• 1• (2• − 4) 3•

I don't but, you still hit my phone up

1• 1• 2• (3• − 1) 5• 3• 3

And baby I'll be movin' on

5• 5• 4• (4• − 4) 3• 2• 1•

and I think you should be somethin'

1• 2• 3• 1• (2• − 2) 3• 1• 2• 3• 1• (2• − 4) 3•

I don't wanna hold back, maybe you should know that

1• 1• 1• 3• (3• − 1) 3 1• 1• (2• − 4) 2• 2• 1• 1• 1 3 5

My mama don't like you and she likes everyone

1• 1• 1• 3• (3• − 1) 3 1• 1• (2• − 4) 2• 2• 1• 1• 1 3 5

And I never like to admit that I was wrong

5• 4• 3• (2• − 4) 1• 1• 3• (3• − 1) 3

And I've been so caught up in my job,

1• 2• (3• − 4) 4• 3• 2• (2• − 2)

didn't see what's going on

1• 1• 5• (5• − 1) 3 5

But now I know

5• 5• 5• (5• − 4) 4• 4• 3• (2• − 2)

I'm better sleeping on my own

1• 1• 3• (3• − 1) 3

'Cause if you like

3• (2• − 2) 4 1• (3• − 1) (3• − 3) 2•

the way you look that much

1• 1• 2• (2• − 4) 1• 3• 1• (2• − 2) 1• 1• 1 3 5

Oh baby, you should go and love yourself

1• 1• 3• (3• − 1) 3 3• (2• − 2) 4 1• (3• − 1) (3• − 3) 2• 1• 1• 2•

And if you think that I'm still holdin' on to somethin'

(2• − 4) 1• 3• 1• (2• − 2) 1• 1• 1 3 5

You should go and love yourself

5• 3• 5• 3 3• 2• 1• 1• 1 5

5• 3• 5• 3 3• 2• 1• 3• 1 5

5• 3• 5• 3 3• 2• 1• (4• − 4) 3• 2• 1• (1• − 1) 3 5

47: Christian Perri – A Thousand Years

Christian Perri's *A Thousand Years* was the theme song for one of the Twilight Movies. Perri got the inspiration to write the song after reading the Twilight Saga novels, the inspiration being the relationships between Edward, a vampire, and Bella, a human. She then re-recorded the song for the *Twilight: Breaking Dawn Part 2 movie*. The vocals were done by Steve Kazee.

While the song did not break charts like many others on this list, it has become so popular that many people cover it on various musical instruments.

On the Kalimba, here is how to play the 'a Thousand Years' notes.

- NOTES, NUMBERS & LYRICS:

(3°-1°) (3°-1°) (3°-1°) 2° (3°-1°) (3°-1°) (3°-1°) 2° (4°-6) (4°-6) (4°-6)

(E°-C°) (E°-C°) (E°-C°) D° (E°-C°) (E°-C°) (E°-C°) D° (F°-A) (F°-A) (F°-A)

1° 3° 4° 3° 2° 1° 75

C° E° F° E° D° C° BG

(1°-1) 1° 1°

(C°-C) C° C°

Heart beats fast

3° 2° 1° (1°-1) 1° 1°

E° D° C° (C°-C) C° C°

Colors and promises

5° 4° 3° 1° 6

G° F° E° C° A

How to be brave

5° 4° 3° 2° 3° 7 1° 1° 1° 1°

How can I love when I'm afraid to fall

(1°-1) (1°-1) (1°-1)

(C°-C) (C°-C) (C°-C)

3° 2° 1° 1° 5° 3°

E° D° C° C° G° E°

Watching you stand alone

5° 4° 3° 1° 6 5° 4° 3° 2° 3° 7 1° 6

G° F° E° C° A G° F° E° D° E° B C° A

All of my doubt suddenly goes away somehow

(6°-6) (7°-7) (1°°-1°) (7°-7)

(A°-A) (B°-B) (C°°-C°) (B°-B)

One step closer

(3°-1) 5° 3° (3°-1) 5° 3° 6° 5° 2° 1°

(E°-C) G° E° (E°-C) G° E° A° G° D° C°

I have died everyday waiting for you

(3°-1) 5° 3° (3°-1) 5° 3° 6° 5° 2° 1°

(E°-C) G° E° (E°-C) G° E° A° G° D° C°

Darling don't be afraid I have loved you

2° 3° (4°-4) 3° 6

D° E° (F°-F) E° A

For a thousand years

1° 2° 1° 2° 3° (4°-4) 3° 2°

C° D° C° D° E° (F°-F) E° D°

I'll love you for a thousand more

(3°-1) 5° 3° (3°-1) 5° 3° 6° 5° 2° 1°

(E°-C) G° E° (E°-C) G° E° A° G° D° C°

All along I believed I would find you

(3°-1) 5° 3° (3°-1) 5° 3°

(E°-C) G° E° (E°-C) G° E°

Time has brought heart to me

6° 5° 2° 1°

A° G° D° C°

I

have loved you

2° 3° (4°-4) 3° 6

D° E° (F°-F) E° A

For a thousand years

1° 2° 1° 2° 3° (4°-4) 3° 5

C° D° C° D° E° (F°-F) E° G

I'll love you for a thousand more

(1°-1) (2°-2) (3°-3) (2°-2)

(C°-C) (D°-D) (E°-E) (D°-D)

One step closer

(6°-6) (7°-7) (1°°-1°) (2°°-2°)

(A°-A) (B°-B) (C°°-C°) (D°°-D°)

One step closer

(3°-1) 5° 3° (3°-1) 5° 3° 6° 5° 2° 1°

(E°-C) G° E° (E°-C) G° E° A° G° D° C°

I have died everyday waiting for you

(3°-1) 5° 3° (3°-1) 5° 3° 6° 5° 2° 1°

(E°-C) G° E° (E°-C) G° E° A° G° D° C°

Darling don't be afraid I have loved you

2° 3° (4°-4) 3° 6

D° E° (F°-F) E° A

For a thousand years

1° 2° 1° 2° 3° (4°-4) 3° 2°

C° D° C° D° E° (F°-F) E° D°

I'll love you for a thousand more

(3°-1) 5° 3° (3°-1) 5° 3° 6° 5° 2° 1°

(E°-C) G° E° (E°-C) G° E° A° G° D° C°

All along I believed I would find you

(3°-1) 5° 3° (3°-1) 5° 3°

(E°-C) G° E° (E°-C) G° E°

Time has brought heart to me

6° 5° 2° 1°

A° G° D° C°

I have loved you

2° 3° (4°-4) 3° 6

D° E° (F°-F) E° A

For a thousand years

1° 2° 1° 2° 3° (4°-4) 3° 5°

C° D° C° D° E° (F°-F) E° G°

I'll love you for a thousand more

48: Closer – Chainsmokers ft Halsey

The Chainsmokers are an American DJ and production duo who got their breakthrough after releasing the 2014 '#Selfie' song.

Since then, they have been part of several hit songs, mostly focusing on Electronic Dance Music (EDM).

Closer is one of their hit songs. The EDM song topped charts in over ten countries and became the second song in music history to spend 32 weeks in the Hot 100 Top Ten charts. Released in 2016, the song featured vocals from American singer Halsey.

Set to a moderately fast 95 beats per minute tempo, it features a rather complicated chord progression that requires consistent practice to master.

-C2

Hey

F F C2C2 C2 C2 A A G G F

I was doing just fine before I met you

F C2 C2 C2 A A G G A

I drink too much and that's an issue

F F AG

But I'm Ok

C2

Hey

C2 C2 C2 A A A G G F

Tell your friends it was nice to meet them

F A A G G F F C A A

But I hope I never see them again

Pre-chorus 1:

F F F F G G

I know it breaks your heart

F F F F F F F F G G F

Moved to the city in a broke down car and

F F G G

Four years, no calls

F F F F F F F F F G G F

Now you're looking pretty in a hotel bar and

C2 A G F C A G

I, I, I, I, I can't stop

C2 C2A G F C A G

No, I, I, I, I, I can't stop

Chorus 1:

G G A F G G A F G G A F G G F

So baby pull me closer in the back seat of your Rover

F G G F F G G

That I know you can't afford

F G G A F G G F

Bite that tattoo on your shoulder

F G G A F G G A

Pull the sheets right off the corner

F G G A F G G

Of the mattress that you stole

F G G F F G G F

From your roommate back in Boulder

F A A F F G G F

We ain't ever getting older

Post-Chorus:

F A A F F G G A

We ain't ever getting older

F A A F F G G F

We ain't ever getting older

-Intrumental Beat-

FGGF FGGF

FAAF FGGF

FGGF FGGF

FAAF FGGA

FGGA FGGF

FAAF FGGF

FGGF FGGF

FAAF FGGA

Verse 2:

C2

You

C2 C2 C2 A A A G G F

Look as good as the day I met you

C2 C2D2 A A G G A F F A G

I forget just why I left you, I was insane

C2

Stay

C2 C2 C2 AAGG F

And play that Blink-182 song

C2 C2 D2 A A G G A AG

That we beat to death in Tucson, OK

Pre-chorus 2:

F F F F G G

I know it breaks your heart

F F F F F F F F G G F

Moved to the city in a broke down car and

F F G G

Four years, no calls

F F F F F F F F F G G F

Now you're looking pretty in a hotel bar and

G A G F C A G

I, I, I, I, I can't stop

F G A G F C A GF

No, I, I, I, I, I can't stop

Chorus 2: (Repeat Chorus 1 and Post-Chorus)

Chorus 3: (same as Chorus 1)

Post-chorus:

F A AF F G G F

We ain't ever getting older

F F A A F F G G F

(No, we ain't ever getting older)

F A AF F G G F

We ain't ever getting older

F F A AF F G G A

(No, we ain't ever getting older)

F A AF F G G F

We ain't ever getting older

F A AF F G G F

(We ain't ever getting older)

F A AF F G G F

We ain't ever getting older

F F A A F F G A A

(No, we ain't ever getting older)

F A AF F G G F

We ain't ever getting older

F F A A F F G G F

No we ain't ever getting older

49: Memories – Maroon 5

Maroon 5 is an American pop rock band that has been making music since 1994.

Memories is one of their most well-known songs, even though it received mostly negative reviews.

However, the general public received the song well, with the song peaking at number two in the US Billboard Hot 100. It also took the number 1 spot in the international music charts.

The song is a ballad for the lost feeling one gets after losing a loved one. It was inspired by the band's loss of their manager, Jodan Feldstein.

Its relatable message on grief and holding onto memories of a loved one is perhaps why it became a success despite critical negativity.

On the Kalimba, here is how to play its notes.

Number notes

5° 3° 4° 5° 3° 4° 5°

3° 1° 2° 3° 1° 2° 3° 1° 2° 3°

2° 1° 7 6 6 6 6 5 6 5 5

5 6 6 6 6 1° 7

5° 3° 4° 5° 3° 4° 5°

3° 1° 2° 3° 1° 2° 3° 1° 2° 3°

2° 1° 7 6 6 6 6 5 6 5 5

5 5 6 6 6 6 1° 7 7 7 7 1° 1°

Letter notes

G° E° F° G° E° F° G°

E° C° D° E° C° D° E° C° D° E°

D° C° B A A A A G A G G

G A A A A C° B

G° E° F° G° E° F° G°

E° C° D° E° C° D° E° C° D° E°

D° C° B A A A A G A G G

G G A A A A C° B B B B C° C°

50: Blinding Lights – The Weeknd

The Weeknd's Blinding Lights is a synth-pop song released in 2019. The single rose to the top of the Billboard Hot 100 charts in 2020 and became one of the most streamed songs of 2020.

The song is The Weeknd's most successful single worldwide to date.

The song speaks about a lover who, in an intoxicated state, decides to speed to his lover to ward off the feeling of loneliness. However, by the end of the song, the protagonist is walking, with his face bloodied, implying that he may have crashed his car while driving drunk.

The song has a rather fast tempo of 171 beats per minute. However, it translates quite well on the Kalimba.

- 6° 6° 5° 6° 7° 3° 5° 6° 6° 5° 6° 7° 3° 5°

2°° 7° 6° 5° 2°° 7° 6° 5° 6°

3° 2° 3° 2° 3° 3° 2° 3° 2° 3° 2° 2° 3° 6

3° 2° 3° 2° 3° 2° 2° 3° 6 2° 3° 6

2° 3° 2° 3° 2° 3° 3° 2° 3° 2° 3° 2° 2° 3° 6

3° 2° 3° 2° 3° 2° 2° 3° 6 2° 3° 6

2° 3° 2° 3° 2° 3° 3° 5° 6° 7° 3° 5° 6°

3° 5° 6° 7° 3° 5° 6°

3° 5° 6° 7° 3° 5° 6° 4°# 4°# 3°

6° 6° 6° 7° 6° 5° 5° 3° 5°

5° 2°° 7° 6° 5° 2°° 7° 6° 5° 6°

7° 5° 6° 6° 6° 7° 6° 5° 5° 3° 5°

5° 2°° 7° 6° 5° 2°° 7° 6° 5° 6°

6° 6° 5° 6° 7° 3° 5° 6° 6° 5° 6° 7° 3° 5°

2°° 7° 6° 5° 2°° 7° 6° 5° 6°

51: The Cranberries – Zombie

The Cranberries is an alternative rock band that sang their biggest hit song, Zombie, as a protest song following the killing of two young victims in a bombing, which was part of a 30-year-old conflict in Northern Ireland.

The song was released in 1994 to much critical acclaim. Zombie features an aggressive electric guitar sound and large distortions. However, it is a song that many have recreated on the Kalimba.

Here's how to play it on the Kalimba.

- Tune: F to F#

3 5 2° 5

3 5 2° 5

1 5 2° 5

1 5 2° 5

2 5 2° 5

2 5 2° 5

4 5 2° 5

4 5 2° 5

Another

353°27

head hangs lowly

32°(135)1°76

Child is slowly taken

11°57656(42)

52°5652°5354

The violence caused such silence

3°2°72°(135)1°761

Who are we mistaken

1°57 656(24)52°54

But you see it's not me, it's not my family

5° 4° 3° (357)3° 4° 3° 3° 4° 5° (135)3° 4°5°5°

5°4°2°(357)5°4°2°5°(5° 5)6°(2°2)462

In your head, in your head they are fighting

With their tanks and their bombs

5°4°3°(3°357)

and their bombs

3°4°3°

And their bombs, and their guns

3°4°3°(135)3°4°3°

In your head, in your head they are crying

5°5°2°(572°)5°4°2° 5°(5°5)6°(4°4)24646

In your head, in your head

4°4°(3575°)353°

Zombie,

354°6°(5°135)6°5°3°

zombie, zombie-ie-ie

3°4°2°(357)3°4°2°3°4°4°(246)4°4°

What's in your head,

4°(24°)4°(3°357)353°

in your head

354°6°(5°135)6°5°3°

Zombie,

3°4°2°(57)

zombie,

3°4°2°

zombie, eh,   eh,   eh, oh

Bruno Mars

Bruno Mars started his music career in 2004 and has grown to be a beloved pop artist. The American singer, dancer, and producer loves to sing his songs with a retro funk touch.

With over 130 million records sold worldwide, Mars is one of the most successful artists of all time. This then means that his songs are popular to play for many instrumentalists.

Below are some of his songs on the Kalimba.

52: Just The Way You Are

Just The Way You Are is the song that propelled Bruno Mars to worldwide fame and was off his debut album, *Doo-Wops & Hooligans*.

The track, released in 2010, compliments a woman about her beauty, with Bruno Mars telling her that he loves her just as she is and she wouldn't need to change a thing.

The song was an instant hit and became a favorite for many people to cover.

Here is how to play it on the Kalimba

- Letter notes, number notation and lyrics

1°   1°4° 5° 6°

C   CF G A

When I see your face

1°   4° 5°6° 5° 4°5° 4°

C   F GA G FG F

Theres not a thing that I would change

4°4°   5° 6°5°

F F   G A G

be-cause your am-azing

6° 5° 4° 5° 4°

A G F G F

just the way you are

1° 4° 5° 6°

C F G A

when you smile

1° 4° 5° 6° 5° 4° 4° 5°4°

C F G A G F F G F

the whole world stop and stares for a while

1° 4° 4° 5° 6° 5°

C F F GA G

be-cause your a-ma-zing

6° 5° 4° 5° 4°

A G F G F

just the way you are

53: Talking to the Moon

Another hit from Bruno's debut album is Talking to the Moon.

The Pop and RnB song speaks about a failed relationship, with the narrator bemoaning his solitude and sadness.

The song was released in 2011 and has a slow tempo, relying majorly on drum percussions and piano as its main instruments.

The song enjoyed much success outside the United States, topping charts in Brazil and Japan. It has also enjoyed a resurgence after getting featured on TikTok in 2021, leading to it topping charts in Australia and Switzerland.

On the Kalimba, here is how to play it:

‾1 4 3 4 3 4 6
I know you're somewhere out there

1 3 3 3 4 4 3
Somewhere far away

2 5 4 2
I want you back

2 5 4 2.
I want you back

1 4 3 4 3 4 6
My neighbors think I'm crazy

1 3 3 3 4 4 3
But they don't understand

2 5 4 2
You're all I have

2 5 4 2.
You're all I have

27 6 5 3
At night when the stars

3 4 5 4 2
Light up my room

2 6 5 4 3.
I sit by myself

2 3 4 2 1°.7. 6.
Talking to the moon

2 3 4 2 1°.7. 6.
Tryin' to get to you

67, 67, 67 6 5,
In hopes you're on The other side

6 6 1° 1° 2° 6 6 6 4 5 4 2
Talking to me too Or am I a fool

2 6 4 5
Who sits alone

6 5 4 3 4 3 2...
Talking to the moon

1 4 3 4 3 4 6
I'm feeling like I'm famous

3

The talk of the town

2 5 4 2

They say I've gone mad

2 5 4 2

Yeah I've gone mad

1 4 3 4 3 4 6

But they don't know what I know

1 3 3 3 4 4 3

'Cause when the sun goes down

2 5 4 2

Someone's talking back

2 5 4 2

Yeah they're talking back

27 6 5 3

At night when the stars

3 4 5 4 2

Light up my room

I sit by myself

2 3 4 2 1°.7. 6.
Talking to the moon

2 3 4 2 1°.7. 6.
Tryin' to get to you

6 7, 6 7, 6 7 6 5,
In hopes you're on The other side

6 6 1° 1° 2° 6
Talking to me too

6 4 5 4 2
Or am I a fool

6 6 4 5
Who sits alone

6 5 4 3 4 3 2
Talking to the moon

54: It will Rain

It Will Rain was a song that Bruno Mars made for *The Twilight Saga: Breaking Dawn – Part 1* movie.

Released in 2011, the song was a commercial success in the United States, South Korea, and New Zealand. It also did well in Canada.

The track is a pop-soul ballad about the torment of going through a heartbreak, with the protagonist struggling through a breakup.

The song's main instrument is the piano with drum percussions and is set to a moderately fast tempo of 72 beats per minute.

Bruno Mar's haunting vocals add an added solemn emotional feel to the song, and you can recreate the tune of the lyrics on the Kalimba as shown below:

⊦ Tabs:

1 5° 5° 6° 5° 5 4 7 5

3 5 3 5 6° 3° 3° 1

5 5 6° 5° 5 4° 7 5

3° 5° 3° 5° 6° 3° 3° 1

5° 5° 5° 5° 5 4° 7

3° 3 5° 6° 3° 2° 1° 6

3° 3° 5 3° 1 1° 2° 1° 6 4 2 6

3° 3° 3° 2° 1° 2° 5 7 5 3° 7 5 2 4° 5 7 2 3° 2° 1°

1°° 5 1° 7 3 1 5 1 7 5 7 5 3° 7 5 7

1°° 5 1° 7 3 1 5° 1 3° 5 7 5 7 3 5 1°

5° 5° 6° 5° 5 4 7 5

3° 5° 3° 5° 6° 3° 3° 1

5° 5° 6° 5° 5 4 7 5

3° 5° 3° 5° 6° 3° 3° 1

5° 5° 5° 5° 5 4° 7

3° 3 5° 6° 3 2 1° 6

3° 3° 5 3° 1 1° 2° 1° 6 4 2 6

3° 3° 3° 2° 1° 2° 5 7 5

3° 7 5 2 4° 5 7 2 3° 2° 1°

1 5 1° 5 1° 3° 5°

3° 5° 1°°

55: *Versace on the Floor*

24K Magic was Bruno's third studio album that featured many retro RnB and Funk musical sounds.

Versace on The Floor was released as the promotional song of the album, and it featured a slow tempo reminiscent of the 1990 RnB.

Released in November 2016, Versace on the Floor speaks of romance and intimacy, culminating in them dropping their Versace clothes on the floor. The raw sensuality in the song saw it banned in Indonesian daytime radio broadcasts.

The song peaked at 98 in the US Billboard Hot 100 and 73rd at the Canadian Hot 100.

On the Kalimba, here is how to replicate the slow jam.

- Letter notes

D° C° B A D D B

D G A B C° B E G A

D D° C° B A D D D E B

G B C° B E G A

D° D° D° D° E° D° C° B

B B C° A G D A

G A B C° D° G

B A

D G A B C° D° D° B° D°

B D° B E°

E° E° E° E° E°

D° D° E° F° G° E° D° E° D° C°

G G A D° C° B A

E° D° C° B A A B G E

3° 3°

2° 2° 3° 4° 5° 3° 2° 3° 2° 1°

5 5 6 2° 1° 7 6

3° 2° 1° 7 6 6 7 5 3

2 7 3 5 5 5

2° 7 7 7 2° 2° 1° 1° 7 7 6 6 5 7

2 7 3 5 5 5 5

2° 7 7 7 2° 2° 1° 1° 7 7 6 6 5 7

2 7 3 5 5 5

Adele

With over 120 million records sold, Adele is no doubt a beloved figure in the world music scene. A soulful singer with a very strong voice, the British singer is currently riding high on her latest album, *30*.

Her soulful songs have become very popular for many musicians and instrumentalists to cover. Below are some of her works that you can play on the Kalimba.

56: Easy on Me

This song is the lead single from her latest album, *30,* and was released in October 2021 to much public approval.

It was Adele's first track in about five years. It is a minimal song in its instrumentals, featuring a somber piano and sparse bass beats.

Easy on Me expresses nostalgia and regret, with Adele singing to her son and asking him to be kind to her following her struggle with divorce.

Shortly after its release, the song broke records at Spotify and Amazon music for the most song streams in a day and week. It topped charts in the United Kingdom and the US and was top 10 in 36 other countries.

The song was widely covered shortly after its release, and on the Kalimba, here is how to recreate it:

- Letter notes

(C-E-C•) G G• D• B C• (A-C•) G C• D• B C•
(E-G-C•) B C• B C• B (F-A-C•) A

G A C• (C-E-C•) G A C• G A C• (A-C•) A

G A C• (E-G-C•) B C• B C• B (F-A-C•) A

G A C• (C-E-C•) C• D• E• G A C• (A-C•) A

G A C• (E-G-C•) B C• B C• B (F-A-C•) B C• B C•

E• (F-A-C•-E•) D• E• D• E• D• (F-A-F•) E•

C• (C-E-G•) E F• E• F• E• D• (A-C•-E•) E• E• (G-B) D• D• E•

(E-G) C• C• D• (F-A) E• C•

(C-E) C• C• D• (F-A) E• C• A G C•

(C-E-G•) E F• E• F• E• D• (A-C•-E•) E• E• (G-B) D• D• E•

C• (E-G-C•) C• D• (F-A) E• C•

(C-E-C•) C• D• (F-A) E• C•

C• C• (C-F•) E• F• E• F• E• F• E• F• E• (A-F•) E• F• E• F• E•
C•

C• (E-G) D• E• D• D• C• (F-A)

(C-A•) G• E A• G• G• E• D•

A C• C• A• G• F• E• G• E D• C• D•

C• D• E• D• D• D• C• A F

C• C• C• C• C• E• G• G•

F A C• A C• F• A•

C• (C-E-G•) E F• E• F• E• D• (A-C•-E•) E• E• (G–B) D• D• E•

(E–G) C• C• D• (F–A) E• C•

(C–E) C• C• D• (F–A) E• C• A G C•

(C-E-G•) E C•• A• G• (A-C•-E•-G•) E• G• (G–B) A•

C• (E-G-C•) C• D• (F–A) E• C•

(C-E-C•) C• D• (F–A) E• C•

F• F• (C–F•) E• C• C• C• E• A

G C• D• B C• (E-G-C•) B C• B C• B

(F-A-C•) A

Number notes

(1-3-1•) 5 5• 2• 7 1• (6-1•) 5 1• 2• 7 1•

(3-5-1•) 7 1• 7 1• 7 (4-6-1•) 6

5 6 1• (1-3-1•) 5 6 1• 5 6 1• (6-1•) 6

5 6 1• (3-5-1•) 7 1• 7 1• 7 (4-6-1•) 6

5 6 1• (1-3-1•) 1• 2• 3• 5 6 1• (6-1•) 6

5 6 1• (3-5-1•) 7 1• 7 1• 7 (4-6-1•) 7 1• 7 1•

3• (4-6-1•-3•) 2• 3• 2• 3• 2• (4-6-4•) 3•

1• (1-3-5•) 2 4• 3• 4• 3• 2• (6-1•-3•) 3• 3• (5-7) 2• 2• 3•

(3-5) 1• 1• 2• (4-6) 3• 1•]

(1-3) 1• 1• 2• (4-6) 3• 1• 6 5 1•

(1-3-5•) 3 4• 3• 4• 3• 2• (6-1•-3•) 3• 3• (5-7) 2• 2• 3•

1• (3-5-1•) 1• 2• (4-6) 3• 1•

(1-3-1•) 1• 2• (4-6) 3• 1•

1• 1• (1-4•) 3• 4• 3• 4• 3• 4• 3• 4• 3• (6-4•) 3• 4• 3• 4• 3• 1•

1• (3-5) 2• 3• 2• 2• 1• (4-6)

(1-6•) 5• 3 6• 5• 5• 3• 2•

6 1• 1• 6• 5• 4• 3• 5• 3 2• 1• 2•

1• 2• 3• 2• 2• 2• 1• 6 4

1• 1• 1• 1• 1• 3• 5• 5•

4 6 1• 6 1• 4• 6•
1• (1-3-5•) 2 4• 3• 4• 3• 2• (6-1•-3•) 3• 3• (5-7) 2• 2• 3•

(3-5) 1• 1• 2• (4-6) 3• 1•]

(1-3) 1• 1• 2• (4-6) 3• 1• 6 5 1•

(1-3-5•) 3 1•• 6• 5• (6-1•-3•-5•) 3• 5• (5-7) 6•

1• (3-5-1•) 1• 2• (4-6) 3• 1•

(1-3-1•) 1• 2• (4-6) 3• 1•

4• 4• (1-4•) 3• 1• 1• 1• 3• 6

5 1• 2• 7 1• (3-5-1•) 7 1• 7 1• 7

(4-6-1•) 6

57: *Someone Like you*

Someone Like You is off Adele's second studio album, *21*.

Released in 2011, the track was a huge success, with Adele's vocal performance receiving exceptional praise. It topped charts in 19 countries and was top 10 in many other regions.

The song speaks of the protagonist's slow acceptance of her failed relationship, wishing her ex the best, telling him that she will find 'Someone like You.'

The song is accompanied only by a piano. On the Kalimba, here is how to play it:

$\vdash$ (6-3) 1° 3° 1° 6 1° 3° 1°

(3-5) 1° 3° 1° 5 1° 3° 1°

(4-1) 1° 4° 1° 4 1° 4° 1°

(6-2) 2° 4° 2° 6 2°

3° 6 1° 7 6 3 3° 3° 1°

7 6 (4-1) 3° 3° 1°

7 6 2 3° 3° 1° 7 6

3° 1° 7 6 (5-4°) 1° 6

7 6 (6-4) 4 6

4 4 4 (2-7) 6 7 1°

3° 6 1° 4° 3° 3° (3°-5) 2° 1°

1° 1° 4 6 4

3 4 (2-7) 6 7 7 6 7 1°

1° 3 1° 1° 1° 7 7 6 (4-7) 7 6 7 6

6 2 7 6 7 6 7 6 7 6 7 6

6 6 (3-7) 1° 1° 1° 1°

7 7 6 7 6 7 6 7 1° (4-2)

6 7 6 7 1° 2 3

6° 6° 6° 6° 5° 3 5° 6° 4 4° 2

4° 5° (6-6°) 3° 3° 6° 5° 3

5° 6° (4-4°) (6-6°)

1^{oo} 1^{oo} (6-1^{oo}) 1^{oo} 3^{oo} 1^{oo} 3

2^{oo} 1^{oo} 7° 6° (4-1^{oo}) 1^{oo} 1^{oo} (7°-2) 6° 4°

58: When we Were Young

Released in 2015, When We Were Young is a song off Adele's Third studio album, 25.

The soulful ballad is a song where the protagonist reminisces memories with a loved one during their young days.

The song was top ten in several countries and, despite never getting an official music video, still managed to shake up charts in the UK and US.

The song features a strong bass with drums and guitar instrumentals. Adele's vocals start off low and husky before soaring in the climax.

On the Kalimba, you can recreate the song melody as shown below:

- Tabs:

1' 1' 1' 1' 7 1' 7 5 6 1 3 5 1

5 5 1' 1' 1 3 5 1

1 1 1 3

(1'6-3)

1' 1' 1' (3'-7) 7 7 7 1' 1' 1 3

1' 1' 1' 2' 2 2'

1' 1' 1' 1'

(3'-1) (4-2') (1'-3)

1' 1' 1' 1' (3'-3) 1' 7 7 1' 1' 1 3

1' 1' 1' 2' 2 2'

1' 1' 1' (572')

1' 3' 2' 1' 2' 6 (35)

3' 2' 1' 2' (57)

1' 3' 2' 1' 2' 6 1 1

3' 2' 1' (72') 5

5' 5' 5' 4' 3' 5' 5' 4' 3' 3

5' 5' 4' 4' 3' 3' 3 2'

1' 2' 3' 1

5' 5' 5' 4' (3'-3)

5' 5' 4' 4' 3' 3' 2'

5' 5' 5' 3' 3' 3' 3' 4'

3' 3' 3' 3' 3' 1'

1' 2' 3' 2' 1' 2' 6

1' 2' 3' 2' 1' (572')

(1'6-3)

1' 1' 1' 1' 7 1' 7 5 6 1 3 5

5 5 1' 1' 5

1 1 1 3

(3'-1) (4-2') (1'-3)

1' 1' 1' (3'-7) 7 7 7 1' 1'

1' 1' 2' 3' 1' 1' 2' 2' 2'

1' 3' 2' 1' 2' 6 1 1

3' 2' 1' (572')

1' 3' 2' 1' 2' 6 6

3' 2' 1' 2' (5'-572')

5' 5' 5' 1 4' 3' 5' 5' 4' 3' (35)

5' 5' 4' 4' 3' 3' (4-2') 1' 2' 3' 1

5' 5' 5' 4' 3' 5' 5' 4' 4' 3' 3' 2'

5' 5' 5' 3' 3' 3' 3' 4'

3' 3' 3' 3' 3' 1'

1' 2' 3' 2' 1' 2' 6

1' 2' 3' 2' 1' 2'

(1'-5) (1'-4') (3'-5) 3'

(1'-5) (1'-4') (3'-5) 3'

(1'-5) (1'-4') (3'-5) 3'

(1'-5) (1'-4') (3'-5) 3' (572')

1' 1' 3' 1' 1' 2' 3' 1'

2′ 3′ 1′ 6 5 1′ 1′ 6 5

3′ 2′ 2′ 1′ 1′ 3′ 5 5

5 5 3′ 2′ 2′ 1′ 2′ 3′ 1′

2′ 3′ 1′ 6 6 1′ 1′ 6 5

3′ 2′ 2′ 1′ 3′ 2′ 2′

1′ 3′ 2′ 1′ 2′ 6 1 1

3′ 2′ 1′ 2′ (5 7)

1′ 3′ 2′ 1′ 2′ 6 1 1

3′ 2′ 1′ 2′ (5′-5 7 2′)

5′ 5′ 5′ 4′ 3′ 5′ 5′ 4′ 3′

5′ 5′ 4′ 4′ 3′ 3′ 2′ 1′ 2′ 3′

5′ 5′ 5′ 4′ 3′ 5′ 5′ 4′ 4′ 3′ 3′ 2′

5′ 5′ 5′ 3′ 3′ 3′ 3′ 4′

3′ 3′ 3′ 3′ 3′ 1′

5′ 5′ 5′ 3′ 3′ 3′ 3′ 4′

3′ 3′ 3′ 3′ 3′ 1′

1′ 1′ 3′ 2′ 1′ 2′ 6

1′ 1′ 3′ 2′ 1′ 2′

1′ 2′ 7

59: Hello

Another song off Adele's 25 album, Hello, was a massive hit worldwide, debuting as number one in the Billboard Hot 100 charts.

The piano ballad lyrics are about the protagonist being nostalgic about a former lover and wishing they could get in touch with them.

The song was such a massive hit that its lyrics became part of an internet challenge, where people hit up their former lovers with lyrics of the song, sometimes to hilarious effects.

It currently stands as one of the best-selling digital singles of all time.

It also got covered in several languages and even in various genres of music, from reggae, rock to traditional folk songs.

And you can also cover it on the Kalimba, as shown below.

- 1 5 3 1 5 3 2 3

2° 2°2°2° 5 3

1° 3°3° 3° 3° 1 2°2°

1° 2° 5 3° 2° 6 1° 4

1° 1° 3° 2° 1° 1

2°2°2° 5 4

1° 3°3° 3° 3° 1 2°2°

1° 2° 5 3° 2° 6 1° 4

2° 3° 1 2°2°2°2° 5 4

1° 3° 3°3°3° 1 2° 1° 2° 5

3° 2° 6 1° 4 1° 1° 3° 4° 1° 1

1° 5° 5 3° 4 3° 2° 1° 1° 3° 5 4°|

6° 1°° 4 2°°2°°2°° 1

3°° 2°° 5 2° 2°2°2° 6° 1°°

4 2°°2°°2°° 1 3°° 2°° 5 1°°

2°° 1°° 3°° 4 6° 1°°1°° 1

$$1^{oo}\ 3^{oo}\ 4$$

$$6^{o}\ 1^{oo}1^{oo}\ 1\ 7^{o}\ 6^{o}\ 5\ 5\ 5\ 5\ 6^{o}\ 1^{oo}$$

$$4\ 2^{oo}2^{oo}2^{oo}\ 1\ 3^{oo}\ 2^{oo}\ 5\ 2^{o}2^{o}2^{o}$$

$$6^{o}1^{oo}\ 4\ 2^{oo}2^{oo}2^{oo}\ 3^{oo}\ 2^{oo}\ 5$$

$$1^{oo}\ 2^{oo}\ 1^{oo}\ 3^{oo}\ 4\ 6^{o}\ 1^{oo}1^{oo}\ 1\ 7^{o}\ 6^{o}\ 5$$

$$6^{o}\ 5^{o}\ 2^{o}\ 1^{o}\ 1$$

Hello – Adele – Letter Kalimba Tabs and Kalimba Notes

C G E C G E D E

D° D°D°D° G E

C° E°E° E° E° C D°D°

C° D° G E° D° A C° F

C° C° E° D° C° C

D°D°D° G F

C° E°E° E° E° C D°D°

C° D° G E° D° A C° F

D° E° C D°D°D°D° G F

C° E° E°E°E° C D° C° D° G

E° D° A C° F C° C° E° F° C° C

C° G° G E° F E° D° C° C° E° G F°

A° C°° F D°°D°°D°° C

E°° D°° G D° D°D°D° A° C°°

F D°°D°°D°° C E°° D°° G C°°

D°° C°° E°° F A° C°°C°° C

B°° A°° G A° D°° C°° E°° F

A° C°°C°° C B° A° G G GG A° C°°

F D°°D°°D°° C E°° D°° G D°D°D°

A°C°° F D°°D°°D°° E°° D°° G

C°° D°° C°° E°° F A° C°°C°° C B° A° G

A° G° D° C° C

Taylor Swift

Taylor Swift started her singing career as a country music singer before transitioning to pop and pop-rock, and now, her discography spans multiple genres.

The singer is well known for her narrative songs that are often inspired by her personal life, usually her breakups and how she deals with them.

With over 200 million records sold, she is one of the best-selling artists to have ever lived. This means most of her songs are popular among instrumentalists.

Below is how to play some of her music on our Kalimba.

60: *All Too Well*

All Too Well is from Taylor Swift's fourth studio album, Red. Released in 2021, the song combined soft rock, country rock, folk, and arena styles in a fusion that made the song a unique sound by Taylor.

The song is about a romantic relationship and its subsequent ending, with Taylor Swift receiving praise for the vivid imagery she used in the lyrics.

On the Kalimba, here is how to play the song:

Numbers:

1 3 3• 2• 2 5 3• 1•

3 6 3• 4 6

1 3 3• 2• 2 5 3• 1• 3 6 3• 4 6

(1-1•) 1• 1• 1• 5 5 2 5 2• 2• 2•

1• (3-3•) 3• 3• 3• 2• 1• 4 1 4 1•

1• 1• 1 1• 1• 1• 5 5 1• (2-2•) 2• 2•

1• 3• 3 2• 1• 1• 1• 1• 4 1 4 4 1•

1 3 3• 2• 2 5 3• 1• 3 6 3 4 1 6

1• 1• (1-1•) 1• 6 1• 5 5 2• (2-2•) 2• 2•

1• (3-3•) 3• 3• 3• 2• 1• 1• 4 1 4 1•

(1-1•) 6 1• 1• 6 1• 5 (2-2•) 2• 2• 1• 2•

1• 3• 3 2• 2• 1• 1• 1• 1• 4 1 4 1•

1• 1• (1-1•) 1• 5• 2• 1•

1• (1•-5•) 5• 2• 1• 1•

1• 1• (6-1•) 5• 2• 1• 1• 6

5 5• 4• 4• 3• 6 4 (5-7) (6-1•)

1• (1-5•) 5• 5• 5• 5• 1• 1• (5-5•) 5• 5• 5•

1• (6-5•) 5• 5• 5• 5• 3• 3• 3• (4-3•) 2• 2• 1• 1•

1• 1• 2• 3• 1 1• 2• 3• 1• 2• 3• 5 2• 2• 3• 7 1•

(4-6) (5-7) (6-1•) (2-7-2•) (3-1•-3•) (4-2•-4•)

1• (1-5•) 5• 5• 5• 5• 1• 1• (5-5•) 5• 5•

(6-5•) 5• 5• 5• 5• 1• 5• 5• (4-5•) 4• 4• 3• 4• 3•

1• 2• 3• 1 1• 2• 3• 1• 2• 3• 5 2• 2• 3• 7

(6-1•) 2• (4-6)

1• 1• 2• 3• 1 1• 2• 3• 1• 2• 3• 5 2• 2• 3•

1• 2• 3• 6 1• 2• 3• 1• 5• 5• (4-5•) 4• 4• 3• 4• 3•

1• 2• 3• 1 1• 2• 3• 1• 2• 3• 5 2• 2• 3• 7

(6-1•) (1-4-6)

Letters:

C E E• D• D G E• C•

E A E• F A

C E E• D• D G E• C• E A E• F A

(C-C•) C• C• C• G G D G D• D• D•

C• (E-E•) E• E• E• D• C• F C F C•

C• C• C C• C• C• G G C• (D-D•) D• D•

C• E• E D• C• C• C• C• F C F F C•

C E E• D• D G E• C• E A E F C A

C• C• (C-C•) C• A C• G G D• (D-D•) D• D•

C• (E-E•) E• E• E• D• C• C• F C F C•

(C-C•) A C• C• A C• G (D-D•) D• D• C• D•

C• E• E D• D• C• C• C• C• F C F C•

C• C• (C-C•) C• G• D• C•

C• (C•-G•) G• D• C• C•

C• C• (A-C•) G• D• C• C• A

G G• F• F• E• A F (G-B) (A-C•)

C• (C-G•) G• G• G• G• C• C• (G-G•) G• G• G•

C• (A-G•) G• G• G• G• E• E• E• (F-E•) D• D• C• C•

C• C• D• E• C C• D• E• C• D• E• G D• D• E• B C•

(F-A) (G-B) (A-C•) (D-B-D•) (E-C•-E•) (F-D•-F•)

C• (C-G•) G• G• G• G• C• C• (G-G•) G• G•

(A-G•) G• G• G• G• C• G• G• (F-G•) F• F• E• F• E•

C• D• E• C C• D• E• C• D• E• G D• D• E• B

(A-C•) D• (F-A)

C• C• D• E• C C• D• E• C• D• E• G D• D• E•

C• D• E• A C• D• E• C• G• G• (F-G•) F• F• E• F• E•

C• D• E• C C• D• E• C• D• E• G D• D• E• B

(A-C•) (C-F-A)A

61: *Love Story*

Love Story was off Taylor Swift's second studio album, *Fearless*.

The song is a narrative whose plot is based on Romeo and Juliet, told from the perspective of Juliet. However, unlike the play, Love Story has a happy ending.

The song is a mid-tempo country-pop song with a slow-building melody that makes it great for the Kalimba.

- Letter notes

(CE G) A° C° A° C° A° C° A°

(CE G) A° C° A° C° A° C° A°

(CE G) A° C° A° C° A° C° A°

(CE G) A° C° A° C° A° C° A° C°

(C° C E G) C° C° C° C° C°

(B° F D) C° D° C° (C° CEG)

C° C° (C° CEG) C° (B° F D)

C° D° C° B C° A F A C° C° C°

B° G G A A A E° D° C° (C° C E G)

C° C° C° C° C° (B° F D) C° D° C°

(C° CEG)C° C° (C° CEG) C° (B° F D)

C° D° C° B C° A F A C° C° C° B°

G G A A A E° D° (C° C E) C° C°

(C° C E G) C° (B° F) D C° D° C°

C° (C° C E) D° C° C° C° (G° D)

F° E° E° (E° C E G) E° E° E° C°

(D° F D) D° D° C° (F E°) E° E° E°

C° (C° C E G) F° E° C° (C° C E G)

D° D° C° E° C° D° (C° D) D° E° D°

(C° C E G) D° D° C° E° C° D°

(C E°) D° C° E° D° C° D° C° E° D°

(C° C E G°) C D (E° E°) E° E° D°

E° E° C C° (C° C E G)

3° 1° (2° 4 2) 2° 2° 1° (4 3°)

3° 3° 3° 1° (1° 1 3 5) 4° 3° 1°

(1° 1 3 5) 2° 2° 1° 3° 1° 2° (1° 2)

2° 3° 2° (1° 1 3 5) 2° 2° 1° 3° 1°

2° (1 3°) 2° 1° 3° 2° 1° 2° 1° 3°

2° (1° 1 3 5°) 1 2 (3° 3°) 3° 3°

2° 3° 3° 1 1° (1° 1 3 5)

62: *Safe & Sound ft The Civil Wars*

Safe & sound was featured in *The Hunger Games* movie as the official soundtrack for the 2021 film.

The song received praise for the simplicity of its music and won the Best Song Written for Visual media at the 2013 Grammy Awards.

The song is set to a moderately slow tempo of 72 beats per minute and usually pairs well with an acoustic guitar.

- (6 1° 3°) 3° 2° 2° 1° 1° (3 5 7) 5 (4 6 1°) 6 5 5 (1 3 5)

(6 1° 3°) 3° 2° 2° 1° 1° (3 5 7) 5 (4 6) 1°

(6 1° 3°) 3° 2° 2° 2° 4° 3° 5° (4 6 1°) 6 5 5 (1 3 5)

(6 1° 3°) 3° 2° 2° 1° 1° (3 5 7) 5 (4 6) 1° 2° 3° 6

(4 6) 1° 2° 3° 6

(2 4) (6 1°) (7 2°) (1° 3°) (3° 5°)

3° 2° 3° 2° 1° (4 6)

(6 1°) (7 2°) (1° 3°) (3° 5°)

3° 2° 3° 2° 1° (4 6)

(6 1°) (7 2°) (1° 3°) (3° 5°)

2° 3° 2° 1° (4 6) (5 7)

(4 6) 1° 2° 3° 6

(4 6) 1° 2° 3° 6

63: *Wildest Dreams*

Wildest Dreams is off Taylor's fifth studio album 1989, released in 2014.

The song is about Taylor Swift as a lover begging her former lover, whom she describes as 'bad but who loves her so well,' not to forget her following the end of their relationship. The song is a ballad that features an atmospheric production and a lush of string instruments.

On the Kalimba, here is how you will play it:

- 1° 1° 1° 1° 2° 1° 2° 3°

3° 3° 6 6 5 5 3° 3° 6 6 5

1° 1° 1° 1° 2° 1° 2°

3° 3° 3° 6 6 5 2° 3° 1° 6°

6 6 3° 6 6 6 6 3° 6 6 3°

1° 1° 2° 1° 2° 3° 2° 1° 6°

6 6 3° 6 6 6 3°|1° 2° 3° 2° 1° 5

1° 2° 1° 2° 1° 2°

2° 3° 2° 1° 2° 6 2° 3° 2° 1° 2° 6 1°

1° 2° 1° 2° 1° 2°

2° 3° 2° 1° 2° 6 2° 3° 2° 1° 2° 6 1°

1° 5 3° 2° 5° 1° 6

1° 5 3° 2° 5° 1° 6

1° 1° 1° 1° 2° 1° 2° 3°

3° 3° 6 6 5 5 3° 3° 6 6 5

1° 1° 1° 1° 2° 1° 2°

3° 3° 3° 6 6 5 2° 3° 1° 6°

6 6 3° 6 6 6 6 3° 6 6 3°

1° 1° 2° 1° 2° 3° 2° 1° 6°

6 6 3° 6 6 6 3° 1° 2° 3° 2° 1° 5

1° 2° 1° 2° 1° 2°

2° 3° 2° 1° 2° 6 2° 3° 2° 1° 2° 6 1°

1° 2° 1° 2° 1° 2°

2° 3° 2° 1° 2° 6 2° 3° 2° 1° 2° 6 1°

1° 5 3° 2° 5° 1° 6

1° 5 3° 2° 5° 1° 6

6 6 1° 3° 6 6 1° 3° 3° 1° 5

6 6 1° 3° 6 6 1° 3° 3° 1° 5

6 6 1° 3° 6 6 1° 3° 3° 1° 5

6 6 1° 3° 6 6 1° 3° 3° 1° 5

3° 1° 5°

1° 2° 1° 2° 1° 2°

2° 3° 2° 1° 2° 6 2° 3° 2° 1° 2° 6 1°

1° 2° 1° 2° 1° 2°

2° 3° 2° 1° 2° 6 2° 3° 2° 1° 2° 6 1°

1° 2° 1° 2° 1° 2°

2° 3° 2° 1° 2° 6 2° 3° 2° 1° 2° 6 1°

1° 2° 1° 2° 1° 2°

2° 3° 2° 1° 2° 6 2° 3° 2° 1° 2° 6 1°

1° 5 3° 2° 5° 1° 6

64: Blank Space

Another song from 1989, Blank Space, was released in 2014.

Taylor Swift wrote the song as a reference to her public persona, which is that she is a flirtatious woman with short, whirlwind romantic relationships.

The song is an electropop with a small hip-hop influence.

-4444444
56654545(42)
4444444
5665541441166
1441166
14416654
444444
56655455(42)
4444444
5665544144
166111441166
144466
77777777777
44444456
444446334

4 4 4 4 4 5 6

4 4 4 4 4 6 3 3 4

1° 1° 1° 7 6 7 6 5

5 5 5 7 6 (5 4)

1° 1° 1° 7 6 7 5

4 7 7 7 1°

4 4 4 4 4 5 6

4 4 4 6 3 3 4

4 4 4 4 5 6 4

4 4 4 6 3 3 4

1° 1° 1° 7 6 7 6 5

5 5 5 7 6 (54)

4 5 5 4 5 5 (54) 2

1 6 4 4 4

Katy Perry

Katy Perry is an American singer who started her career in gospel music in her teens.

After an unsuccessful debut album, Katy Hudson, Perry moved to Los Angeles and got into secular music, where she also adopted the Katy Perry moniker.

Since then, she has become one of the best-selling artists of all time, selling over 143 million records. Thus, her songs make for great Kalimba cover music.

65: Firework

Firework is a dance-pop empowerment anthem released in 2010 from Perry's third studio album, *Teenage Dream.*

The song reached number 1 in the Billboard Hot 100 and was praised for Perry's vocals, but its lyrics and production were panned.

Still, the song is widely covered on many instruments, and here is how it looks on the Kalimba:

- Letters Notation:

B D°D° BB GAA GG GAA GG GAA BB B D°D° BB GAA GG

GAA GG GGA BB D° G°G° D°D° D°D°D° E°G°G° E°G°G°

E°E° D°E° D°D° B E°D°D° B D°D° BB GAA GG GAA GG

GAA GG B AC° BD° C°E° G°G° D°A° G°B°G°E° D°°C°°B°

A°A° G°B° D°°C°°B° A°A° G°E° D°°C°°B° A°A° A°A° D°

D°°C°B° A°A° G°E° D°°C°°B° A°A° G°B° D°°C°°B° A°A°

G°E° D°°C°°B° A°A° A°A° D° D°°C°B° A°A° G°E°

Numbers Notation:

7 2°2° 77 566 55

566 55 566 77

7 2°2° 77 566 55 566 55

556 77 2° 5°5° 2°2° 2°2°2° 3°5°5°

3°5°5° 3°3° 2°3°

2°2° 7 3°2°2°

7 2°2° 77 566 55

566 55

566 55 7 61° 72° 1°3°

2°°1°°7° 6°6° 5°7°

2°°1°°7° 6°6° 5°3°

2°°1°°7° 6°6° 6°6°

2° 2°°1°7° 6°6° 5°3°

2°°1°°7° 6°6°

5°7° 2°°1°°7° 6°6° 5°3°

2°°1°°7° 6°6° 6°6°

2° 2°°1°7° 6°6° 5°3°

66: The One That Got Away

This song was off Perry's *Teenage Dream* album and is a mid-tempo love ballad about lost love.

The One That Got Away peaked at number three in the Billboard Hot 100 and was one of the songs that were a major hit in 2012.

On the Kalimba, here is how you can play it:

- Number notes

(1) 2° 2° 2° 2° 2° 1° 5 2° 2° 2°

5 2 (3) 2° 2° 2° 2° 1° 5 2° 2° 2° 2°

6 (6) 2° 2° 2° 2° 2°

1° 2° 3° 2° 1° 7 (4) 6

5 5 (1) 2° 2° 2° 2°

2° 1° 5 2° 2° 2° 2°

(3) 2° 2° 2° 2° 2° 1°

5 2° 2° 2° 2°

(6) 2° 2° 2° 2° 2° 1°

2° 3° 2° 1° 7 (4) 6

4° 4° 4° 3° (135) 3°

4° 4° 4° 3° (357) 2°

4° 4° 4° 3° (61°) 3°

2° 1° 2° 3° 2° 1° 7 (4) 6

4° 4° 4° 3° (135) 3°

4° 4° 4° 3° (357) 2°

4° 4° 4° 3° (61°) 3°

2° 1° 2° 3° 2° 1° 7 (4) 6

6 6 6 5 5 (135)

Letter notes

(C) D° D° D° D° D° C° G D° D° D°

G D (E) D° D° D° D° C° G D° D° D° D°

A (A) D° D° D° D° D°

C° D° E° D° C° B (F) A

G G (C) D° D° D° D°

D° C° G D° D° D° D°

(E) D° D° D° D° D° C°

G D° D° D° D°

(A) D° D° D° D° D° C°

D° E° D° C° B (F) A

F° F° F° E° (CEG) E°

F° F° F° E° (EGB) D°

(AC°) E°

D° C° D° E° D° C° B (F) A

F° F° F° E° (CEG) E°

F° F° F° E° (EGB) D°

F° F° F° E° (AC°) E°

D° C° D° E° D° C° B (F) A

A A A G G (CEG)

67: *Never Worn White*

Never Worn White was released as a standalone single in 2020. The accompanying music video was also when Perry announced her pregnancy

The song did not enter the Billboard Hot 100 but still received relative airplay in European countries.

The song is a piano ballad with a soft production and heartfelt lyrics and chorus.

FCA-F GE G-EF DCB-D

BCE-G DEDC-C EGECE BAE

EDC C-CABC

A BBDA B   .

C D-(C-D-F-A) BAE

EE DCC-CBCE

B CB DC D A CE

CED CC-CBCE

BC BDBCD E EGBAE

BED CE-C D

C C-CAB BCA-C

B C CB CB

CEBC C B-D

BC CB C D E EG

BC CB CB

BCED BCA-C

BC G-CEG GE CE

C D G-CEG GE CE

DE G-CGFG

A-(C-D-F-A) C D DFA

BC G-CEGGE CE

C D G-CE GAE EG

D EG-CGFG A-(C-D-F-A)

CD DFA CC CEGEC-C|

68: *Hot n cold*

Hot n Cold was off Perry's second studio album, One of the Boys.

Released in 2008, the song lyrics speak about an unstable romantic relationship caused by the partner's mood swings, with the lyrics speaking of the protagonist's confusion over their partner's behavior.

The song is a pop ballad featuring strong guitars and synthesizers, set at a moderately fast tempo of 132 beats per minute.

- Tuning: 4 to 4#

7 7 5 6
You change your mind

6 5 6 6 5 3
Like a girl changes clothes

2 7 7 5 6
Yeah you, PMS

6 5 6
Like a b°tch

6 5 3
I would know

2 7 7 5 6
And you over think

6 5 6

Always speak

6 5 3

Cryptically

2 2 7

I should know

5 6 5 6 5 6 5 3

That you're no good for me

2 2 5 5 5 5

'Cause you're hot then you're cold

2 5 5 5 5

You're yes then you're no

2 6 6 7 3

You're in then you're out

2 6 6 7 3

You're up then you're down

2 5 5 5 5

You're wrong when it's right

You're in then you're out

2 6 6 7 3
You're up then you're down

2 5 5 5 5
You're wrong when it's right

2 5 5 5 5
It's black and it's white

2 6 6 7 3
We fight, we break up

2 6 6 7 3
We kiss, we make up

7 7 7 7 7 7 6 6
You don't really want to stay, no

3 6 6 6 6 6 6 5 5
But you don't really want to go

2 5 5 5 5
You're hot then you're cold

2 5 5 5 5
You're yes then you're no

You're in then you're out

2 6 6 7 3

You're up then you're down

3° 7 5 5 3° 7°

Someone call the doctor

1° 1° 1° 1° 1° 1° 7 6 7

Got a case of a love bipolar

5 5 3° 7 5 5 3° 7

Stuck on a roller coaster

1° 1° 1° 7 4 5 6

Can't get off this ride

7 7 5 6

You change your mind

6 5 6 6 5 3

Like a girl changes clothes

2 2 5 5 5 5

'Cause you're hot then you're cold

2 5 5 5 5

You're yes then you're no

You're in then you're out

2 6 6 7 3
You're up then you're down

2 5 5 5 5
You're wrong when it's right

2 5 5 5 5
It's black and it's white

2 6 6 7 3
We fight, we break up

2 6 6 7 3
We kiss, we make up

2 5 5 5 5
You're hot then you're cold

2 5 5 5 5
You're yes then you're no

2 6 6 7 3
You're in then you're out

2 6 6 7 3
You're up then you're down

You're wrong when it's right

2 5 5 5 5
It's black and it's white

2 6 6 7 3
We fight, we break up

2 6 6 7 3
We kiss, we make up

7 7 7 7 7 7 6 6
You don't really want to stay, no

3 6 6 6 6 6 6 5 5
But you don't really want to go

2 5 5 5 5
You're hot then you're cold

2 5 5 5 5
You're yes then you're no

2 6 6 7 3
You're in then you're out

2 6 6 7 3
You're up then you're down

69: *Chained to the Rhythm*

Chained to the Rhythm is off Perry's fifth studio album, Witness.

The song is a pop and disco song with a danceable beat and catchy chorus, but with lyrics that raise social awareness on the mechanical nature of modern life. It is set to a moderate tempo of 95 beats per minute.

Chained reached number one in several countries outside the US but was top five in the US, Germany, Belgium, and many other European countries.

-

Chained to the Rhythm - Katy Perry Number Notation

6 (1-6) (1-6) (1°-6°) (7-5°) (7-5°) (7-5°) 6 (1°-6°) (1-6) (1°-6°)
(7-5°) (7-5°)

3° 5° 6° 3° 3°

Are we crazy?

1° 7° 6° 5° 3° 2° 2°

Living our lives through a lens

10° 7° 6° 5° 3° 2° 2°

Trapped in our white picket fence 1° 3° 2° 2°

Like ornaments

1° 3° 3° 3° 3° 3° 3° 3° 3° 5° 3° 5° 3°

So comfortable, we're living in a bubble, bubble 1° 3° 3° 3°
3° 3° 3° 3° 3° 5° 3° 5° 3°

So comfortable, we cannot see the trouble, trouble 3° 5° 6°
3°

Aren't you lonely?

107° 6° 5° 3° 2° 2°

Up there in utopia

3° 3° 10° 7° 6° 5° 3° 2° 2°

Where nothing will ever be enough

1° 3° 2° 2°

Happily numb

1° 3° 3° 3° 3° 3° 3° 3° 3° 5° 3° 5° 3°

So comfortable, we're living in a bubble, bubble 1° 3° 3° 3°
3° 3° 3° 3° 3° 5° 3° 5° 3°

So comfortable, we cannot see the trouble, trouble

5° 3° 1° 2° 2° 1° 2° 3° 3°

So put your rose-colored glasses on

1° 2° 77

And party on

5° 6° 6° 3° 3° 3° 6° 6°

Turn it up, it's your favorite song 6° 6° 6° 3° 3° 3° 6° 6° 5° 6°

Dance, dance, dance to the distortion

5° 6° 6° 4° 4° 4° 6° 6°

Turn it up, keep it on repeat

6° 6° 6° 6° 6° 4° 4° 4° 6° 6° 5° 6° 6°

Stumbling around like a wasted zombie, yeah 4° 4° 6° 6°

We think we're free

6° 4° 4° 6° 6°

Drink, this one's on me

70: Daisies

Daisies is off Perry's Smile album, her sixth. Released in 2020, the song is an electropop that mostly features acoustic guitars, with a moderately fast tempo of 122 beats per minute.

The song celebrates the strength to overcome adversity, inspired by her time in quarantine at the onset of the COVID-19 pandemic.

Here is how to play it on the Kalimba:

- 5 5 6 7 5 6 (1 3)

5 5 6 7 5 6 (1 3)

7° 6 5° 4 (3° 1) 3 4° 4° 5° 3° (1° 1)

5 5 6 7 5 6 (1 3)

5 5 6 7 5

5° 6° 7° (6° 1°) 7° 6° 5° (3° 1) 3° 4° 4° 5° 3° (1° 1)

5 5 6 7 5 6 (1 3)

5 5 6 7 5 6

2 (4 5) (1 3)

5 5 6 7 5 6

2 (4 5) (1 3)

5 5 6 7 5 6

(1 2) 4° 4° 4° 5° 3° (1° 1)

4° 4° 4° 3° 1° (1 5)

4° 4° 4° 5° 3° (1° 1)

4° 4° 4° 3° 1° (1 5)

2° 4° 3° 4° 5° (1° 3 5)

2° 4° 3° 4° 5° (1° 3 5)

2° 3° 4° 3° 5° 1° (7 2° 4°) (7 2° 4°) (7 2° 4° 6°)

(1 2) 4° 4° 4° 5° 3° (1° 1)

5 2° 4° 4° 4° 3° 1° (1 5)

2 4° 4° 4° 5° 3° (1° 1)

5 4° 4° 4° 3° 1° (1 5)

2° 4° 3° 4° 5° (1° 3 5)

2° 4° 3° 4° 5° (1° 3 5)

2° 3° 4° 3° 5° 1° (7 2° 4°) (7 2° 4°) (7 2° 4° 6°)

71: Senorita – Shawn Mendes ft Camila Cabello

Senorita is a love ballad released in 2019 and shot to number 1 in the Billboard Hot 100.

The love ballad, set to acoustic and Spanish guitar strums, speaks about two friends, played by Camilla and Mendes, who can't keep their hands off each other.

The song is set to a moderate tempo of 117 BPM and is easy to recreate on the Kalimba.

CAE CBG GCBA BC AE CBG

G CBAGF CCC EE BBB

B CB CBG

BCBABC AE CBG

BCBAG F CCC EE BBB

B CB CBG B CB CB AA GA

EDED C EDED CCBA

EDED C EDEF EDC A EEE

GG DDD CB

EDED C EDED CCBA

EDED C EDEF EDC A EEE

GG DDD

A EGF EDC AEGF

A EGF EDC EE

EFEDEF CA FEC

EFEDC A EEE GG DDD

EFEDEF CA FEC

EFEDC A EEE GG DDD

B CB CBG B CB CD CBA|

72: *Someone You Loved – Lewis Capaldi*

Scottish Singer Lewis Capaldi released this song in 2018 from his third studio album, Breach.

The song was a commercial success, topping the UK Singles Charts and becoming one of the best-selling singles of 2019.

The song is about loss, coming to Capaldi after losing his grandmother. The slow and moody melody of the song makes it perfect for kalimba practice.

- Numbers notes

6° 1° 6° 1° 6° 1° 6° 1° 3° 5 3° 5 3° 5 3° 5

4° 6 4° 6 4° 6 4° 6 2° 4 2° 4 2° 4 2° 4

1° 1° 6 1° 6 1° 6 2° 3° 2° 1° 1° 2° 1° 6 5

1° 1° 6 1° 6 1° 6 2° 3° 2° 1° 1° 2° 1° 6 5

5 6 5 5 3° 5 6 5 3° 2°

5 5 5 5 1° 3° 3° 2° 1°6

5 6 5 5 3° 5 6 5 3° 2°

3° 3° 3° 3° 2° 2° 2° 2° 1° 1° 2°

1° 1° 1° 4° 4° 3° 1° 1° 4° 4° 3°

1° 1° 4° 4° 3° 1° 1° 1° 5° 5° 3°

1° 1° 4° 4° 3° 1° 1° 1° 1° 4° 4° 3°

3° 3° 3° 3° 2° 2° 2° 2° 1° 1° 1° 2° 1°

6° 6° 6° 6° 5° 5° 3° 3° 2° 2° 3° 4° 3° 2° 1°

6° 6° 6° 6° 5° 5° 3° 3° 2° 2° 3° 4°

1° 1° 4° 4° 3° 1° 1° 4° 4° 3°

1° 1° 4° 4° 3° 1° 1° 1° 5° 5° 3°

1° 1° 4° 4° 3° 1° 1° 1° 4° 4° 3°

3° 3° 3° 3° 2° 2° 2° 2° 1° 1° 1° 2° 1°

Letter notation

A° C° A° C° A° C° A° C° 3° G E° G E° G

F° A F° A F° A F° A D° F° D° F D° F D° F

C° C° A C° A C° A D° E° D° C° C° D° A G

C° C° A C° A C° A D° E° D° C° C° E° A G

G A G G E° G A G E° D°

G G G G C° E° E° D° C° A

G A G G E° G A G E° D°

E° E° E° E° D° D° D° D° C° C° D°

C° C° C° F° F° E° C° C° F° F° E°

C° C° F° F° E° C° C° C° G° G° E°

C°

C° F° F° E° C° C° C° C° F° F° E°

E° E° E° E° D° D° D° D° C° C° C° D° C°

A° A° A° A° G° G° E° E° D° D° E° F° E° D° C°

A° A° A° A° G° G° E° E° D° D° E° F°

C° C° F° F° E° C° C° F° F° E°

C° C° F° F° E° C° C° C° G° G° E°

C° C° F° F° E° C° C° C° F° F° E°

E° E° E° E° D° D° D° D° C° C° C° D° C°

Billie Eilish

Billie Eilish is an American singer who gained public attention in 2015 with Ocean Eyes' debut.

Eilish has usually presented herself publicly in baggy clothes and colorful hairstyles. Her fashion sense and music have made her an influential person among the young generation.

Considered one of the most successful artists of the 2010s, Eilish's songs also make for great covers on the Kalimba.

73: *Lovely*

Lovely is one of Eilish's most successful singles. Featuring singer Khalid, the song was part of the soundtrack to the Netflix hit, 13 Reasons Why.

The song is described as a pop ballad, with Eilish and Khalid trying to overcome depression together.

The track features piano and violin strings and percussions, all of which are minimalist.

On the Kalimba, here is how to play it:

Kalimba Songbook

Lettered Notation:

A° C°°A° C°°A° C°°A° C°°A° C°°A° C°°A° C°°A°

E° G°A° B° G°A°

F° E° D° F° E° C°° 8°

D° E° E° D° D° D° E° E° D° D° C° A BAGE

BC D° E° E° D° D° B C° D° E° E° D° D° C

E D° E° D° C° A B C D° E° G° A° G° E° D° E° D° C° A B C D E° G°A° G° E°

D° E° D° C° A B C D E° G° A° G° E° D° E° D° C° A B C° D° E° G°A° G° E°

E° D° C° BAD° C BE° D° C° BABAC

E° D° C° BAD° C° BABC BBAC

D° E° E° D° D° E° D° E° E° D° D° D° C° ABAGE BC° D° E° E° D° D° B C° D° E° E° D° D° C

ED° E° D° C A B C D° E° G° A° G° E° D° E° D°C° A B C D E° G°A° G° E°

D° E° D° C° A B C D° E° G° A° G° E° D° E° D° C° A B C D E G°A° G° E°

E° D° C° BAD° C BE° D° C BABAC°

E° D° C BAD° C BBC BBAC

G°A° G° E° F° E° D° BE ABC BC° B A F° E° A C° B

E° D° C° BAD° C BE D° C° BABAC E° D° C BAD° C BABC BBAC BAGA.

$-\,2^{\circ}\,3^{\circ}\,3^{\circ}\,2^{\circ}\,2^{\circ}$

$6\,7\,6\,5\,3$

$1^{\circ}\,1^{\circ}\,2^{\circ}\,3^{\circ}\,3^{\circ}\,2^{\circ}\,2^{\circ}$

$2^{\circ}\,3^{\circ}\,3^{\circ}\,2^{\circ}\,1^{\circ}$

$2^{\circ}\,3^{\circ}\,2^{\circ}\,1^{\circ}\,6\,7\,1^{\circ}\,2^{\circ}\,3^{\circ}\,6^{\circ}\,5^{\circ}\,3$

$2^{\circ}\,3^{\circ}\,2^{\circ}\,1^{\circ}\,6\,7\,1^{\circ}\,2^{\circ}\,3^{\circ}\,6^{\circ}\,5^{\circ}\,3$

$2^{\circ}\,3^{\circ}\,2^{\circ}\,1^{\circ}\,6\,7\,1^{\circ}\,2^{\circ}\,3^{\circ}\,6^{\circ}\,5^{\circ}\,3$

$2^{\circ}\,3^{\circ}\,2^{\circ}\,1^{\circ}\,6\,7\,1^{\circ}\,2^{\circ}\,3^{\circ}\,6^{\circ}\,5^{\circ}\,3$

$3^{\circ\circ}\,2^{\circ\circ}\,1^{\circ\circ}\,7^{\circ}\,6^{\circ}\,2^{\circ\circ}\,1^{\circ\circ}\,7^{\circ}$

$3^{\circ\circ}\,2^{\circ\circ}\,1^{\circ\circ}\,7^{\circ}\,6^{\circ}\,7^{\circ}\,6^{\circ}\,1^{\circ\circ}$

$3^{\circ\circ}\,2^{\circ\circ}\,1^{\circ\circ}\,7^{\circ}\,6^{\circ}\,2^{\circ\circ}\,1^{\circ\circ}\,7^{\circ}$

$7^{\circ}\,1^{\circ\circ}\,7^{\circ}\,7^{\circ}\,6^{\circ}\,1^{\circ\circ}$

74: Ocean Eyes

The song that put Eilish in the limelight, Ocean Eyes, was released in 2015 and later re-released in 2016. It was part of her self-made album, *Don't Smile at Me.*

The song received positive reviews, entered the Billboard Hot 100, and peaked at 84 and 72 in the UK Singles Chart.

The song is a pop and RnB ballad with sparse percussions and low bass, set to 145 beats per minute.

- (3° 1 3 5) 2° (3 5 7)

(3° 1 3 5) 2° (3 5 7)

(3° 1 3 5) 2° (3 5 7)

(3 5 7) 2° (1 3 5)

(3° 1 3 5) 2° (3 5 7) 6 5

(3° 1 3 5) 2° (3 5 7)

(3° 1 3 5) 2° (3 5 7)

6 5 6 (3 5 7) 2° (1 3 5)

(3° 1 3 5) 2° (3 5 7) 6 5

(3° 1 3 5) 2° (3 5 7)

(3° 1 3 5) 2° (3 5 7)

6 5 6 (3 5 7) 2° (1 3 5)

6 5 6 (3 5 7) 2° (3° 1 3 5)

7° 5° 1 2 3

6° 5° 6° 5° 1 2 3

3 3 3 7 7 7 6 6 6 5 3

3 4 5 6 5 (3 5 7) 2° (1 3 5)

7 5 1 2 3

6° 5° 6° 5° 1 2 3

3 3 3 7 7 7 6 6 6 5 3

3 4 5 6 5 (3 5 7) 2° (1 3 5)

6 5 6 (3 5 7) 2° (3° 1 3 5)

(3° 3) (5° 5) (7° 7)

(3° 3) (5° 5) (7° 7)

(7° 7) (2°° 2) (3° 1 3 5)

Billie Eilish

Ocean eyes

E-C D-D (EGB) x3

(G-B) D-D (C-E)

E-C D-D (EGB) AG

E-C D-D (EGB)

E-C D-D (EGB) D

GA (G-B) D-D (C-E)

E-C D-D (EGB) AG

E-C D-D (EGB)

E-C D-D (EGB) D G

A (G-B) D-D (C-E)|

A D-(G-B) D-D E-C

AGC DE

AGC-AGDE

EEEB-C B B B D-AA G-E

AGCDE

AGC-AGDE

EEEB-C BBB D-AA G-E

EEEGEG B-G D-B E-C

A B-G D-B C-E

75: *When the Party is Over*

This song was released in 2018 and was the second single from Eilish's debut studio album *When We All Fall Asleep, Where Do We Go?*

The song is a piano ballad with bass backgrounds, with Eilish vocals standing out in the track.

The song is composed in the C# minor, and on the Kalimba, you will lay it as shown below.

- [Verse 1]

1 2 3 2 3 2 3 5

5 (6 1) 5 (6 1) 5 (6 1) 5 (6 1) 1'

(1' 1) 2' (3' 1 3) 2' (3' 1 3) 2' (3' 1 3) 5'

5' (6' 2 4) 5' (6' 2 4) 5' (6' 2 4) 5' (6' 2 4) 1"

[Chorus]

1" 7' 6' 7' 6' 5' (3' 1) 3 5' (3' 1) 3 2' (1' 1) 3 5 3

1' 2' 3' (4' 4) 3' 4', 2' (3' 3) 2' 3' (4 6 1'), (3' 1) 2' 3' 1' (6 1 3)

1' 2' 3' (4' 4) 3' 4', 2' (3' 3) 2' 3' (4 6 1'), (3' 1) 2' 3' 1' (6 1 3)

[Verse 2]

1 2 3 2 3 2 3 5

5 (6 1) 3 5 (6 1) 3 5 (6 1) 3 5 6 1'

(1' 1) 3 2' (3' 1) 3 2' (3' 1) 3 2' (3' 1) 5'
5' (6' 2) 4 5' (6' 4) 6 5' (6 4) 6 5' (6 4) 1"

[Chorus]
1" 7' 6' 7' 6' 5' (3' 1) 3 5' (3' 1) 3 2' (1' 1) 3 5 3
1' 2' 3' (4' 4) 3' 4', 2' (3' 3) 2' 3' (4 6 1'), (3' 1) 2' 3' 1' (6 1 3)
1' 2' 3' (4' 4) 3' 4', 2' (3' 3) 2' 3' (4 6 1'), (3' 1) 2' 3' 1' (6 1 3)

[Bridge]
6 1' (6 1 3), 5 5 3 5 (1 3)
6 1' 6 1' 6 3' (3' 1 3)
(2' 2 4) 3'(1' 1) 7 (6 1)
(2' 2 4) 3'(1' 1) 7 (6 1 3)

[Chorus]
1" 7' 6' 7' 6' 5' (3' 1) 3 5' (3' 1) 2' (1' 1) 3 5 3

1' 2' 3' (4' 4) 3' 4', 2' (3' 3) 2' 3' (4 6 1'), (3' 1) 2' 3' 1' (6 1 3)
1' 2' 3' (4' 4) 3' 4', 2' (3' 3) 2' 3' (4 6 1'), (3' 1) 2' 3' 1' (6 1 3)

When the party is over

CDE DE DC CDE DG DC

CDE DE DEG

GA GA GA GA C

DE DE DE DEG

CA GA GA GAC

CBA BA GE GE GD

CDE FE FD EDEC EDE CA x2

CAC CA GG

AC AEE DCD

CD CE DCB DE CBA

CBA BA GE GE GD|

CDE FE FD EDEC EDE CA x2

76: Everything I Wanted

The track was released in November 2019 to critical acclaim over its musical production and lyrics.

The song is a house and electronica pop song, with minimal piano and a downtempo bass guitar. It speaks of her strong relationship with her brother and songwriter, O'Connell, and how overprotective he is of her.

E° C° D°

E° B E°

C° D° E° F° E° C°

B D°

B E° C°

E° D° C° B

(B B) G° F° E°

F° (F° F° F°)

E° D° C° B

B G° F° E°

F° F° E° D° E°

D° C° B C° A

A E° D° C° (B B) G

E° D° C° B (B B) G°

F° E° (F° F°) E° E°

G° F° E° D° B

B E° A

C° D° E° G° A° A°

B° G°

E° C° D°

E° B E°

C° D° E° F° E° C°

B D°

B E° C°

E° D° C° B

(B B) G° F° E°

F° (F° F° F°)

E° D° C° B

B G° F° E°

F° F° E° D° E°

D° C° B C° A

A E° D° C° (B B) G

E° D° C° B (B B) G°

F° E° (F° F°) E° E°

G° F° E° D° B

B E° A

C° D° E° G° A° A°

B° G°

G° A° G° F° F° E°

G° A° (A° A°) B° G°

F° G° G° (F° F°) E°

A° A° C°° A° B°

G° D°°

C°° B° B° C°° A°

(G° G°) A° (A° A°) B°

G° G°

E° G° D° F° E°

77: *Happier Than Ever*

Released in 2021, the song drew heavy inspiration from Eilish's self-reflection during the pandemic.

The song has a sparse jazz influence, with electropop arrangements of minimal acoustic guitar and a meditative tempo.

Eilish reflects on the challenges women go through in the entertainment industry, from emotional abuse, power struggle, misogyny, and self-consciousness.

- Tabs+Lyrics:

_____

When I'm away from you

3 (3°5) 7 (12°) 3 5 1° (13)

_____

I'm happier than ever

5 5 6 7 1° (357) 3 7 3 (62)

_____

Wish I could explain it better

6 5 6 7 1° 2° (1°3) 5 1° 3 (57)

_____

I wish it wasn't true, mmm

6 6 7 1° 2° (61°3°) 2° (3°5) 2° (57)

_____

Give me a day or two

5 (3°5) 7 (12°) 3 5 1° (13)

—————————

To think of something clever

5 5 6 7 1° (357) 3 7 3 (62)

—————————

To write myself a letter

6 6 7 1° 2° (1°3) 5 1° 3 (57)

—————————

To tell me what

6 6 7 1° 2° (61°3°) 2° (3°5) 2° 1° (572°) 1° (42°)

—————————

to do, mm-mm

7 (1°1) 3 5 3 (1°135)

—————————

Do you read my interviews?

3° 2° (1°1) 3 5 1° 2° (1°3°) 2° (1°5)

—————————

Or do you skip my avenue?

3° (357) 3 5 7 7 1° (72°) (1°7)

—————————

When you said you were passin' through

2° (62) 2 5 6 7 (61°) 7 6

—————————

Was I even on your way?

7 1° (41) 6 1° 2° (572°)

— — — — — — — — —

I knew when I asked you to (When I asked you to)

3° 2° (1°1) 3 5 1° 2° (1°3°) 2° (1°5)

— — — — — — — — —

Be cool about what I was tellin' you

3° (357) 3 6 7 6 7 1° (72°) 1° 7

— — — — — — — — —

You'd do the opposite of what you said you'd do (What you said you'd do)

2° (62) 5 6 5 6 5 6 7 (61°) 7 6

— — — — — — — — —

And I'd end up more afraid

7 1° (41) 6 1° 2° (572°)

— — — — — — — — —

Don't say it isn't fair

3° 2° 1° (357) 1° 5 7

— — — — — — — — —

You clearly weren't aware

6 7 1° (572°) 3° (52°) 1°

— — — — — — — — —

that you made me miserable, ooh

2° (63) 7 1° 6 (61°3°) 2° 3° 5° (6°61°3°)

— — —

—————————

So if you really wanna know
1° 2° 3° (4°4) 3° 2° 1° (357)

—————————

When I'm away from you (When I'm away from you)
5 (3°5) 7 (12°) 3 5 1° (13)

—————————

I'm happier than ever (I'm happier than ever)
5 5 6 7 1° (357) 3 7 3 (62)

—————————

Wish I could explain it better (Wish I could explain it better)
6 5 6 7 1° 2° (1°3) 5 1° 3 (57)

—————————

I wish it wasn't
6 6 7 1° 2° (61°3°) 2° (3°5) 2° 1° (572°) 1° (42°)

—————————

true, mmm
7 (1°135)

78: O Holy Night (Christmas Carol)

O Holy Night is a beloved Christmas Carol originally based on a French-language poem written by Placide Cappeau. John Sullivan Dwight did the English version.

The song reflects on the birth of Jesus. The slow melody makes the song a pleasure to play on the Kalimba, especially if you are still learning to play the instrument.

- Numbered Notation:

3 4 3 (1 3 5)

5 (4 6 1°) 6 4 6 (1° 1 3 5) (3 5)

5 4 3 (1 3 5)

3 4 (3 5) 4 2 (1 3 5)

3 4 3 (1 3 5)

5 (4 6 1) 6 4 6 (1° 1 3 5) (3 5)

5 4 3 (7 7°) 5 6 (7 7°) 1 7 (3 5)

5 (5 1) 6 (3 5)

5 6 5 (1° 1 3) (4 1) (6 1) (3 5)

5 (5 1) 6 (3 5)

6 5 (1° 1) (4 1) (6 1) (3 5)

1° 7 6 7

7 (2 2°) 6 7 6 (1° 3 5) 1°

(1° 1) (3 3°) (2° 2) 5 (1° 1 3 5)

7 6 (1 3 5) 5 6 5 (5 1)

1° 2° 5 (5° 5 7) (4 4°)

(3° 3) (2 2°) (1° 1)

7 1° 2° (1° 1 3)

Lettered Notation:

E F E (C E G)

G (F A C°) A F A (C° C E G) (E G)

G F E (C E G)

E F (E G) F D (C E G)

E F E (C E G)

G (F A C) A F A (C° C E G) (E G)

G F E (B B°) G A (B B°) C B (E G)

G (G C) A (E G)

G A G (C° C E) (F C) (A C) (E G)

G (G C) A (E G)

A G (C° C) (F C) (A C) (E G)

C° B A B

B (D D°) A B A (C° E G) C°

(C° C) (E E°) (D° D) G (C° C E G)

B A (C E G) G A G (G C)

C° D° G (G° G B) (F F°)

(E° E) (D D°) (C° C)

B C° D° (C° C E)

79: Girls Like You – Maroon 5 ft Cardi B

Maroon 5 released the song in 2017 off their sixth studio album, *Red Pill Blues*. They also featured high-flying rapper Cardi B in a second version of the song —the song went on to become a mega-hit.

The version featuring Cardi B went straight to the top of the Billboard Hot 100 charts, spending seven weeks at number one.

The song is a pop-rock set to C major and a 125 BPM tempo.

$$- 1' \, 1' \, 1' \, 3' \, 2' \, 1'$$
$$1' \, 1' \, 3' \, 2' \, 1' \, 2' \, 2'$$
$$1' \, 1' \, 1' \, 5' \, 1'$$
$$1' \, 1' \, 5' \, 1' \, 2' \, 2'$$
$$1' \, 1' \, 2' \, 3' \, 5$$
$$5 \, 5 \, 3' \, 5 \, 2' \, 2'$$

$$1' \, 1' \, 2' \, 2' \, 5' \, 5'$$
$$1' \, 2' \, 2' \, 5' \, 5'$$
$$5' \, 2' \, 2' \, 1'$$

$$1' \, 1' \, 2' \, 3'$$
$$1' \, 1' \, 1' \, 7 \, 1' \, 2'$$

6 6 6 6 1′ 2′

6 6 6 6 1′ 2′ 1′ 1′

1′ 1′ 2′ 3′

1′ 1′ 1′ 7 1′ 2′

6 6 6 6 1′ 2′

6 6 6 6 1′ 2′ 1′ 1′

1′ 1′ 1′ 7 7 7 7 6

1′ 1′ 2′ 3′

1′ 1′ 1′ 7 7 7 7 6

Coldplay

Coldplay is one of the world's most well-known and beloved rock bands. The British band, made up of four members, is one of the most successful bands, with over 100 million records sold.

Their songs have received many covers, and the Kalimba can cover Coldplay songs.

80: Fix You

Fix You is off Coldplay's 2005 third studio album, X&Y.

The song was a huge hit, reaching number 4 in the UK Singles Charts.

The song features an organ accompanied by piano and guitar in its first half, with electric and bass guitar and drums picking up in the song's second part.

- 5 5 (3° 1) 3° 1° 5 5 (1° 3) 1° 7 (6 1) (2 5)

5 5 (3° 1) 3° 1° 5 5 (1° 3) 1° 7 (6 1) (2 5)

5 5 (3° 1) 3° 1° 5 (3 5 7) 1° 7 (6 1) (2 5)

5 1° 2° (3° 1) 3 5 (5° 3) 1° (1° 6) (5 7)

5 5 (3° 1) 3° 1° 5 (1° 3) 1° 7 (6 1) (2 5)

5 5 (3° 1) 3° 1° 5 (1° 3) 1° 7 (6 1) (2 5)

5 5 (3° 1) 3° 3° 3° 4° (3° 3) 2° (2° 2) (1° 6) (5 7)

5 1° 2° (3° 1) 3 5 (5° 3) 1° (1° 6) (5 7) (6 4 1)

4° (3° 3) (2 5 7 2°) 1° 7 6 5 (6 4) 1° (4 1)

4° (3° 3) (2 5 7 2°) 1° 7 6 5 (6 4) 1°

(4 1) (1° 6 4) (3° 3) (2 5 7 2°) 7 (3° 3) 1°

1 3 1° 3 3° 7° 6 3° 1°°

5 3° 7° 1° 3° 1°° 3 3° 7°

6 3° 1°° 5 2° 7 (1° 1 3 5)

81: The Scientist

Off their second album, A Rush of Blood to the Head, The Scientist is built around a piano ballad.

The lyrics tell the story of a man who desires to love and a sense of powerlessness in its presence.

The song also features string arrangements, with a harmony acoustic guitar backing slow tempo drums and bass guitar riffs.

- F G F C° A

4541°6

come up to meet you,

F G F C°A

4541°6

tell you i'm sorry,

F F G F AA G AGF

1454666654

you don't know how lovely you are.

F G F C° A

4541°6

i had to find you,

F G F C° A

4541°6

tell you i need you,

F G F A A GAGF

1454666654

tell you i set you apart.

F G F C°A

4541°6

tell me your secrets,

F F G F C°A

4541°6

and ask me your questions,

F G F A A A AGF

454666654

oh let's go back tot he start.

FG F C°A

4541°6

running in circles,

FG F C°A

4541°6

coming up tails,

F G F AA AGF

454666654

heads on a science apart.

F°D°C° F° D° C° F°C°

4°2°1°4°2°1°4°2°

nobody said it was easy,

61°62°666654

it's such a shame for us to part.

F°D°C° F° D° C° F°C°

4°2°1°4°2°1°4°2°

nobody said it was easy,

A C C°A D A A A G FE

661°62°6666543

no one ever said it would be this hard.

Bb Bb Bb Bb Bb C BbAF

7777764

oh, take me back to the start.

16542 16542 (46)

ooooooooooooooooooooooooooooo

F G F CA F FG F CA

i was just guessing at numbers and figures,

FG F AA AAGF

pulling the puzzles apart.

FG F FCA

questions of science,

science and progress,

F F G F A A AAGF

don't speak as loud as my heart.

F F G F C A

and tell me you love me,

F G F C A

come back and haunt me,

F G F A A A AGF

oh and i rush to the start,

FG F CA

running in circles,

FG F CA

chasing our tails,

FG F AA AAGF

coming back as we are.

FDC F DC FC

nobody said it was easy,

A C C A D A A A AGF

oh it's such a shame for us to part,

FD

FC

nobody said it was easy.

A C CA C# A A A G FE

no one ever said it would be so hard.

Bb BbBb Bb Bb C BbAF

i'm going back to the start.

CAGFDC

oh,

CAGFDC~

oh~

CAGFDC

oh~

CAGFDC~

oh~

82: Yellow

Yellow is off Coldplay's debut studio album, *Parachutes*, released in 2000.

The song reached number 4 in the UK Singles Chart and was Coldplay's first-ever top-five hit in the UK.

It is Coldplay's most famous song and has been widely covered. Despite the brightness and hope reflected in its title and cover, the song lyrics are open to interpretation. The song is about being in a state of unrequited love.

The song has a moderately slow tempo of 88 BPM

- Letter notes

B B A B

B B A B B A

G A G A B G

E G E G E D C

B B A B

B B A B B A

G A G A B G

E G E G E D C

BBABBA

GAGABG

EGEGEDC

G E° D

GGDDBBG

G E° E° D G G

D D B B G G G E°

D G G D D B B (C E G)

G G D D B B (C E G)

Letter notations

776777677

656567535

353217767

7767765656

753535353217

7677656567

2 5 5 2 2 7 7 5 5 3°

3° 2 5 5 2 2 7 7 5

5 5 3° 2 5 5 2 2 7

7 (1 3 5) 5 5 2 2 7 7 (1 3 5)

Yellow - Coldplay easy tabs

Look at the stars

7767 BBAB

Look how they shine for you

77672'6

BBABDA

And everything you do|

56562'5

GAGADG

Yeah they were all yellow

3535532

EGEGGED

I came along

7767

BBAB

I wrote a song for you

77672'6

BBABDA

And all the things you do

56562'5

GAGABG

And it was called "Yellow"

3535553 2

EGEGGED

So then I took my turn

77672'6

BBABDA

Oh what a thing to have done

56562'5

GAGADG

And it was all yellow

3535553 2

EGEGGED

Your skin

53° 2°

GED

Oh yeah, your skin and bones

552° 2° 775

GGDDBBG

Turn into something beautiful

53° 3° 2° 5 5 2° 2° 775

GEED GG DDBBG

You know, you know I love you so

55 3° 2° 5 52° 2° 77 (135)

GGEDGGDDBB (CEG)

You know I love you so

♭552° 2° 77 (135)

GGDDBB (CEG)

83: Hymn for The Weekend

Hymn for the Weekend was off Coldplay's seventh studio album, *A Head Full of Dreams,* and featured Beyoncé.

The track uses a moderate 90 BPM and features piano accompaniments with electric guitar, drums, and drum percussions. All instruments combine to create a dreamy chorus further enhanced by Beyoncé and ChrisMartin's (Coldplay lead vocalist) vocals.

On the Kalimba, the song is as below:

1° 1° 1° 7 6 6 6 6 7 7 7 7 7 7 6 6

1° 1° 1° 7 6 6 6 6 7 7 7 7 7

1° 7 1° 6 1° 7 2° 1° 1° 7 1° 6 1° 7° 2° 1°

1° 7 1° 6 1° 7 2° 1° 5 6 5° 4° 3° 3°

1° 7 1° 6 1° 7 2° 1° 1° 7 1° 6 6 1° 7 2° 1°

1° 7 1° 6 1° 7 2° 1° 5 6 5° 4° 3° 3°

6° 1° 3° 3° 3° 2° 1° 6 1° 3° 4° 4° 3° 2°

6° 1° 3° 3° 3° 2° 1° 6 6 7 7 7 1° 1° 2°

6° 1° 3° 3° 3° 2° 1° 6 1° 3° 4° 4° 3° 2°

6° 1° 3° 3° 3° 2° 1° 6 6 7 7 7 1° 1° 2°

4° 3° 2° 4° 3° 3° 3° 7 7 6 1° 7 2° 1°

4° 3° 2° 4° 3° 3° 3° 7 7 6 1° 7 2° 1° 7 6

84: Red Hot Chili Peppers – Otherside

The Red Hot Chili Peppers is an American Rock band that has been active since 1983. The band has many hit songs under their belt; Otherside is one of them.

Released in 1999 as part of their third studio album, Californication, the song confronts the ugly battle that addicts face with their previous addictions.

The song is a pop-rock/alternative rock set to a moderately fast 123 BPM, with multiple chord progressions. As shown below, you can easily recreate it on the Kalimba with enough practice.

- **Numbered Notation:**

3 3

3 6

6 7 6 5 3 3

3 2 2

2 3 3° 3°

2° 1°

2° 1° 7 1° 5 1° 5

5 3° 2° 1° 7 1° 7 1°

1° 6 1°

1° 7 1° 5 5 5

5 3° 2° 7 1° 7 1° 1°

2° 1° 1°

1° 7 6 5 1° 1° 1°1°

1° 3° 2° 7 1° 7 6 1° (3°1°)

(1° 6°) 1° 1° 1° 1° 1° 7 (3° 7) (5° 7)

3 3 3 3

6 1° (3° 1°) (1° 6°)

1° 1° 1° 1° (1° 5)

7 3° 5° 3 3 3 3 (6 3)

1° (3° 1°) (1° 6°)

1° 1° 1° 1° (1° 5)

7 3° (5° 7)

7 7 7 (57) 7 (72°) (5° 7)

7 (6 7) 1° 3° (6 3)

1° 3° 3°

2° 1° 2° 1° 7 6 5 1° 5

5 3° 2° 7 1° 7 1° 7 1°

1° 6 (1°6)

(1°6)

7 (1°6) (35)(3 5) (3 5)

(3 5) 3°

2° 7 1° 7 1° (1° 3)

2° 1° (1°6)

(1° 6) 7 (1°6) 5 (1° 3 5) 1° 1° (1° 3 5)

(1° 3 5) (3° 7) 2° 7 1° 7 (6 3) 1° (3° 1°) (1° 6°)

1° 1° 1° 1° (1° 5) 7 3° 5° 3 3 3 3

(6 3) 1° 3° (1° 6°) 1° 1° 1° 1° (1° 5) (1° 7) (3° 2°) 5°

3 3 3 3 6 1° (3° 1°) (1° 6°)

1° 1° 1° 1° (1° 3 5) 7 (3° 7) (5° 7)

7 7 7 (2 5 7) 7 (7 2°) (5° 7) 2 2 (2 7)

2 (6 7) 1° (6 3) (6 6°)

3 3 3 3 (5 7) 7 (7 2°) (5° 7) 7 (6 7)

(1° 3) (3° 3) (6 6°)

(5 7) 7 (7 2°) (5° 7)

5 7 2° 5°

(6 7) 1° 3° (6 3)

(6 3) 1° 3° 6°

(1° 3) 3° (3° 1° 3)

2° (1°6)

2° (1° 6) 7 (1° 6) 5 (1° 3 5)

(3 5)

(3 5)

(3° 7)

2° 7 1° 7 (1° 6 3) 7 (1° 6 3)

(1° 3) 6 (1° 6)

(1° 6) 7 (1° 6) (3 5) (3 5) (3 5)

(3 5) (3° 7) 2° (2° 7) 1° (2 7) (1° 3)

(1° 3) (1° 2°) 1° (1° 6)

(1° 6) 7 (1° 6) 5 (1° 3 5) 1° 1° (1° 3 5)

(1° 3 5) (3° 7)

2° 7 1° (2 7) (1° 6 3)

Lettered Notation:

E E

E A

A B A G E E

E D D

D E E° E°

D° C°

D° C° B C° G C° G

G E° D° C° B C° B C°

C° A C°

C° B C° G G G

G E° D° B C° B C° C°

D° C° C°

C° B A G C° C° C°C°

C° E° D° B C° B A C° (E°C°)

(C° A°) C° C° C° C° C° B (E° B) (G° B)

E E E E

A C° (E° C°) (C° A°)

C° C° C° C° (C° G)

B E° G° E E E E (A E)

C° (E° C°) (C° A°)

C° C° C° C° (C° G)

B E° (G° B)

B B B (G B) B (B D°) (G° B)

B (A B) C° E° (A E)

C° E° E°

D° C° D° C° B A G C° G

G E° D° B C° B C° B C°

C° A (C°A)

(C°A)

B (C°A) (EG)(E G) (E G)

(E G) E°

D° B C° B C° (C° E)

D° C° (C°A)

(C° A) B (C°A) G (C° E G) C° C° (C° E G)

(C° E G) (E° B) D° B C° B (A E) C° (E° C°) (C° A°)

C° C° C° C° (C° G) B E° G° E E E E

(A E) C° E° (C° A°) C° C° C° C° (C° G) (C° B) (E° D°) G°

E E E E A C° (E° C°) (C° A°)

C° C° C° C° (C° E G) B (E° B) (G° B)

B B B (D G B) B (B D°) (G° B) D D (D B)

D (A B) C° (A E) (A A°)

E E E (G B) B (B D°) (G° B) B (A B)

(C° E) (E° E) (A A°)

(G B) B (B D°) (G° B)

G B D° G°

(A B) C° E° (A E)

(C° E) E° (E° C° E)

D° (C°A)

D° (C° A) B (C° A) G (C° E G)

(E G)

(E G)

(E° B)

D° B C° B (C° A E) B (C° A E)

(C° E) A (C° A)

(C° A) B (C° A) (E G) (E G) (E G)

(E G) (E° B) D° (D° B) C° (D B) (C° E)

(C° E) (C° D°) C° (C° A)

(C° A) B (C° A) G (C° E G) C° C° (C° E G)

(C° E G) (E° B)

D° B C° (D B) (C° A E)

85: Old Town Road – Lil Nas X ft Billy Ray Cyrus

Old Town Road was Lil Nas X's biggest hit that thrust him to a path of no return in his career.

Released in 2018, the Old Town Road remix was released on April 5 2019, featuring country musician Billy Ray Cyrus. And from here, the song took a life of its own.

The song is described as a country trap song and features strong banjo strums and heavy bass.

The song is set to 68 BPM.

- 6°... 6° 6° 6° 6° 5° 4°

2° 2° 6° 5° 5°

2° 2° 1° 5°

5° 6° 4° 3° 3°

2° 2° 2° 6° 5° 4°

2° 2° 6° 5° 5°

2° 2° 1° 5°

5° 6° 4° 3° 3°

(3° 2)(3° 2)(3° 2)

5 6 6 5 6

4 5 5 4 5

4 5 5 4 5

♭5 4 5 4 5 6 6 5 4 2

5 6 6 5 6

4 5 5 4 5

4 5 5 4 5

4 2 2 5 4 5 6 6 5 4 2

6 6 5 5 6 2° 6 5

4 2 2 2 2 5 4 3 2

6 6 5 5 6 2° 6 5

4 2 2 2 2 5 4 3 2

6°... 6° 6° 6° 6° 5° 4°

2° 2° 6° 5° 5°

2° 2° 1°

5° 5° 6° 4° 3° 3°

2° 2° 2° 6° 5° 4°

2° 2° 6° 5° 5°

2° 2° 1°

5° 5° 6° 4° 2° 2°

Imagine Dragons

Imagine Dragons are an American rock band and one of the most successful rock bands ever.

They have sold over 75 million records and have seen their songs widely covered in various genres. Below, we look at some of their songs on the Kalimba.

86: Thunder

Released in 2017, Thunder was off Imagine Dragon's third studio album, Evolve, released in 2017 and peaked at number 4 at the US Billboard Hot 100.

The song is an electropop song that speaks about pursuing one's dreams. On the Kalimba, here is how to play Thunder;

1 1' 6 1' 3'

1 1 6

1' 3'

1 1 6

1' 3'

1 1' 6 1' 3'

4 1' 6

1' 6

4 6 1 6

1' 6

4 1' 6 1' 6

1'-4 6 4 3

1 1 6 1' 3' 1 1 6 1' 1' 3' 1 1' 6 (6-1')

1' 6 1'-1

1' 6 (6-1')

4 (2-4) 1'

4 4 (2-4) 1'

4 4 (2-4) 1'

4 4 4 (2-4) 1' 1' 5'

1'-1 5'

1'-1 5' 3'

1'-1 5'

1' 1' 1'-1 5' 3' 5'

(4-6) 3'

(4-6) 3' 1'

(4-6) 3'

6 6 (4-6) 3' 2' 1'

1'-1 6

1' 6 1'-1 6. 6 4

1' 1'-1. 1' 6 1'-1 6. 6

1'-1 6

1' 1'-1. 1' 6

1'-1 6

1' (4-6)

1'-1 6 1' 6

87: Demons

Demons is off Imagine Dragons debut album, *Night Visions*.

Released in 2013, the song is about one person warning their loved one of their flaws, hence the title 'Demons,' which is often used to refer to people's major flaws.

The song has a slow to moderate tempo and features telltale pop-rock guitar strums and heavy drums.

- Tune:

3=3b

6=6b

7=7b

3°=3b°

6°=6b°

7°=7b°

337 5 4337 5

4331° 5 4 33666

337 5 4337 5

4331° 5 4 33666

7777 57

7773° 2° 1°

5555 56

3°3°3°3° 3°2°

2°2°2°2° 2°1°

5555 5⁶

6666 55

5°5°7° 3°2°

5°5°7° 2°1°

5°5°5°5° 5°6°

6°6°6°6° 5°5°

5°7°3° 2°

5°7°2°1°

5°5°5° 5°6°

6°6°6°6° 5°5°

3337 5 4337 5

4331° 5 433666

337 5 4 3337 5

4331° 5 433666

7777 57

7773° 2°1°

5555 5⁶

6666 55

3°3°3°3° 3°2°

2°2°2°2° 2°1°

5555 5⁶

6666 55

5°5°7° 3°2°

5°5°7° 2°1°

5°5°5°5° 5°6°

6°6°6°6° 5°5°

5°7°3°2°

5°7°2°1°

5°5°5°5° 5°6°

6°6°6°6° 5°5°

Imagine Dragons

Demons

EEBDFFEEBB

FFEECC

GFEEAGAA

EEBDFFEEBB

FFEECC

GFEEAGAA

DB B BBG BB

BBBED CC

GGGGGAG

AAAAGGD|

EEEEEDB

DDDDDCC

GGGGGAG

AAAAGGD

GG B-DE (B-D)

GG B-BD CC

GG-CGGGCAG

AAAAGGGD

GG-CGGGCAG

AAAAGFDE

88: Believer

Believer was released off Imagine Dragon's Evolve album in 2017 and reached the Billboard Hot 100, peaking at number 4.

The song has 125 BPM and features strong drum beats and heavy electric guitar strums.

The lyrics speak about believing that you can overcome the difficult things happening in one's life.

Letter notes

A E° D° D° C° D° D° E° D° C° A G A

E° D° D° C° D° D° E° D° C° A G A C° A° G° (A C° E°)

E° D° C° A G A C° A° (B D° A#)

A A E° D° D° D° C° D° D° D° E° D° C° A G A

E° E° D° D° C° D° D° E° D° C° A G A C° A° (G° A C° E°)

E° D° C° A G A C° A° (B D° A#)

A A A A A A A

A A A A A A A

C° C° C° C° C° C°

B B B B B B

A A A A A A A

A A A A A A A

C° C° C° C° C° C°

B B B B

(D F A A°)

C°° C°° B° A° C°° C°° B° A° A° C°° C°° B° (B D° A°#)

(D F A A°)

C°° C°° B° A° C°° C°° B° A° A° C°° C°° B° (B D° A°#)

(C E C° E°)

D° D° C° D° C° D° C° D° C° (C E C° E°)

D° D° C° D° C° D° C° D° A

(D F A A°)

C°° C°° B° A° C°° C°° B° A° A° C°° C°° B° (B D° A°#)

A E° D° D° C° D° D° E° D° C° A G A

E° E° D° D° C° D° D° E° D° C° A G A G A C° A° G° (A C° E°)

E° D° C° A G A C° A° (B D° A°#)

A A A A A

A A A A A A A

A A C° C° C° C°

C° C° B B B B B

A A A A A A A

C° C° C° C° C° C°

C° C° C° B°

C° C° B A

(D F A A°)

C°° C°° B° A° C°° C°° B° A° A° C°° C°° B° (B D° A°#)

(D F A A°)

C°° C°° B° A° C°° C°° B° A° A° C°° C°° B° (B D° A°#)

(C E C° E°)

D° D° C° D° C° D° C° D° C° (C E C° E°)

D° D° C° D° C° D° C° D° A

(D F A A°)

C°° C°° B° A° C°° C°° B° A° A° C°° C°° B° (B D° A°#)

A E° D° D° C° D° D° E° D° C° A G A

E° E° D° D° C° D° D° E° D° C° A G A G A C° A° G° (A C° E°)

E° D° C° A G A C° A° (B D° A°#)

C° A A A A A A A

A C° C° C° C° C° C° C°

C° C° B C° C° B A

(D F A A°)

C°° C°° B° A° C°° C°° B° A° A° C°° C°° B° (B D° A°#)

(D F A A°)

C°° C°° B° A° C°° C°° B° A° A° C°° C°° B° (B D° A°#)

(C E C° E°)

D° D° C° D° C° D° C° D° C° (C E C° E°)

D° D° C° D° C° D° C° D° A

(D F A A°)

C°° C°° B° A° C°° C°° B° A° A° C°° C°° B° (B D° A°#)

Number notes|

6 3° 2° 2° 1° 2° 2° 3° 2° 1° 6 5 6

3° 2° 2° 1° 2° 2° 3° 2° 1° 6 5 6 1° 6° 5° (6 1° 3°)

3° 2° 1° 6 5 6 1° 6° (7 2° 6#)

6 6 3° 2° 2° 2° 1° 2° 2° 2° 3° 2° 1° 6 5 6

3° 3° 2° 2° 1° 2° 2° 3° 2° 1° 6 5 6 1° 6° (5° 6 1° 3°)

3° 2° 1° 6 5 6 1° 6° (7 2° 6#)

6 6 6 6 6 6 6

1♭ 1° 1° 1° 1° 1° 1°

7 7 7 7 7 7

6 6 6 6 6 6 6

6 6 6 6 6 6 6

1° 1° 1° 1° 1° 1°

7 7 7 7

(2 4 6 6°)

1°° 1°° 7° 6° 1°° 1°° 7° 6° 6° 1°° 1°° 7° (7 2° 6°#)

(2 4 6 6°)

1°° 1°° 7° 6° 1°° 1°° 7° 6° 6° 1°° 1°° 7° (7 2° 6°#)

(1 3 1° 3°)

2° 2° 1° 2° 1° 2° 1° 2° 1° (1 3 1° 3°)

2° 2° 1° 2° 1° 2° 1° 2° 6

(2 4 6 6°)

1°° 1°° 7° 6° 1°° 1°° 7° 6° 6° 1°° 1°° 7° (7 2° 6°#)

6 3° 2° 2° 1° 2° 2° 3° 2° 1° 6 5 6

3° 3° 2° 2° 1° 2° 2° 3° 2° 1° 6 5 6 5 6 1° 6° 5° (6 1° 3°)

3° 2° 1° 6 5 6 1° 6° (7 2° 6°#)

6 6 6 6 6

6 6 6 6 6 6 6

6 6 1° 1° 1° 1°

1° 1° 7 7 7 7 7

6 6 6 6 6 6 6

1° 1° 1° 1° 1° 1°

1° 1° 1° 7°

1° 1° 7 6

(2 4 6 6°)

1°° 1°° 7° 6° 1°° 1°° 7° 6° 6° 1°° 1°° 7° (7 2° 6°#)

(2 4 6 6°)

1°° 1°° 7° 6° 1°° 1°° 7° 6° 6° 1°° 1°° 7° (7 2° 6°#)

(1 3 1° 3°)

2° 2° 1° 2° 1° 2° 1° 2° 1° (1 3 1° 3°)

(2 4 6 6°)

1°° 1°° 7° 6° 1°° 1°° 7° 6° 6° 1°° 1°° 7° (7 2° 6°#)

6 3° 2° 2° 1° 2° 2° 3° 2° 1° 6 5 6

3° 3° 2° 2° 1° 2° 2° 3° 2° 1° 6 5 6 5 6 1° 6° 5° (6 1° 3°)

3° 2° 1° 6 5 6 1° 6° (7 2° 6°#)

1° 6 6 6 6 6 6 6

6 1° 1° 1° 1° 1° 1° 1°

1° 1° 7 1° 1° 7 6

(2 4 6 6°)

1°° 1°° 7° 6° 1°° 1°° 7° 6° 6° 1°° 1°° 7° (7 2° 6°#)

(2 4 6 6°)

1°° 1°° 7° 6° 1°° 1°° 7° 6° 6° 1°° 1°° 7° (7 2° 6°#)

(1 3 1° 3°)

2° 2° 1° 2° 1° 2° 1° 2° 1° (1 3 1° 3°)

2° 2° 1° 2° 1° 2° 1° 2° 6

(2 4 6 6°)

89: *Bad Liar*

Bad Liar is off Imagine Dragon's 2018 album Origins, the band's fourth studio album.

The song is an alternative and indie rock with strong guitar riffs in the chorus, with the piano playing prominently in the rest of the song.

- 3 1° 1° 1° 7 (3 6) 1° 1° 1° 7 (1 4)

1° 1° 1° 7 (5 1°) 1° 1° 1° 2° (5 7 2°)

3 1° 1° 1° 7 (3 6) 1° 1° 1° 7 (1 4)

1° 1° 1° 7 (5 1°) 1° 1° 1° 2° (5 7 2°)

1° 1° 1° 4° 3° 1 3 6 1° 1° 4° 3° 1 4 6 1

1° 7 1° (1 3 5 1°) 1° 2° 2° 5 2 7

1° 1° 1° 4° 3° 1 3 6 1° 4° 3° 1 4 6 1°

1° 7 1° (1 3 5 1°) 1° 2° 2° 2°

2 5 7 2° 1° 7 (1 3 5 1°)

CD CE CD CE CGE x3

CC EE CCC EE

CC EED CC EED

CCC B BBB D

CCC EE DC CC EE

CEED CC EED

CCC B BBB D

E CCC BA CCC BF

CCC BC CCC DD

E CCC BA CCC BF

CCC BC CCC DD|

CC CC FE CC FE CBC CDD

CC CC FE C FE CBC CCDD

CC EE CCC EE

CC EED CC EED

F FFE GG GAG CFE ED DC

CCC BA CCC BF

CCC BC CCC DD

CCC BA CCC BF

CCC BC CCC DD

CC CC FE CC FE CBC CDD

CC CC FE CC FE CBC CCDD

Beyoncé

Popularly referred to as Queen B, Beyoncé is one of the most successful and influential modern-day artists. Beyoncé started her music career in 1997 as part of the Destiny's Child music group. However, she has continued her success in music after the group split in 2001. Her songs have been widely covered; below are a couple of them.

90: Halo

Halo was off her third album, I Am...Sasha Fierce in 2008. The song was released in 2009; it features strong drums, keyboard, piano, strings, and percussion. It is a pop and RnB ballad with lyrics about love, with Beyoncé expressing her love for her lover in raw and open emotions, with Halo describing the fact that she sees her lover as perfect.

On the Kalimba, here is how to play it:

Beyonce

Halo

1'-1 61' 61'6 1'

71' 2-27272'1'

1'7 65 6-4 46464

67656-446464

6543 (1-31)

31' 1'1' 1'72' (2)

47771'664 (1)

366 66676 (4)

3666 6 21 (3)

31'1'1'1' 72' (76)

76767 61'664 (1)

666666676 3'1' (1)

36 6 6 6 6-3 (1)

6 3' 3' 3' 3' 4' 4' 3' (3)

1'2' 3' 3' 3' 3' 6' 6' 4' (4)

1'2' 3'3' 1'764' (1)

1'2' 3' 3' 3'3' 5' 6' (6) 1" (1)

6' 6' 6' 6' 6' 7' (37)

6' 6' 7' 7' 7' 1" 6' 6' 4' (4)

6' 6' 6' 6' 6' 6' 6' 3' 2' 1' (1)

3' 6' 6' 6' 6' 5' 6' (6-3)

3' 6' 6' 6' 6' 6' 6' 7' (3-7)

6' 7' 6' 7' 6' 1" 7' 6' 6' 5' 4' (4)

6' 6'6' 6' 6' 6' 6' 3'2'1' (1)

3' 6' 6' 6' 6' 5' 6'7'

"1'7 "1"1'7 "1

6' 6' 7' 1" 7' 1" 7' 2" 1" 7"

6' 6' 7' 1" 7' 1" 7' 1" 7" 1"

6' 6' 7' 1" 7' 1" 7' 7' 6' (6' 3" 1")

1" 1" 1" 1" 1" 72" (76)

2" 2" 2" 2" 2" 3" 1" 1" (4)

6' 6' 6' 6' 6' 6' 7' 6 (4)

3'3'3' 6' 6' 6'2' 1' (13)

3' 1" 1" 1" 1" 7' 7'-7 6'

3'7' 1" 1" 1" 1" 7 7-7 (6' 4')

6' 6' 6' 6' 6' 7'6' 4

3'3' 3' 6' 6' 6' 3' 2' 1' 1'(3)

1'3' 3'3' 3'4'4' 3' (3)

1'2' 3' 3'3' 6' 6'7' 1" 7' 6'4"

1'3' 3'3' 6'6' (2'1'7)

1'2' 3'3'3'3' 5' 6' (6) 1" (1)

6' 6' 6' 6' 6' 6' 7' (37)

6'6' 6' 6' 6' 6' 6'3'2' 1'(1)

3'6' 6' 6' 6'5'6' (6-3)

3' 6' 6' 6' 6' 6' 7' (37)|

6' 7' 6' 7' 6' 1" 766 5' 4' (4)

6' 6' 6' 6' 6' 6' 6' 3' 2' 1' (1)

6' 6' 6' 6' 5' 6' 7'

1" 7' 1" 7' 1" 7' 1"

6' 6' 7' 1" 7' 1" 7' 2" 1" 7"

6' 6' 7' 1" 7' 1" 7' 7'6'

1'-16 1'6 1' 61'

71'2-2 72 72'1'

1'7 654-646464

67656-4 46464

654 3 (1-3)

91: *If I Were A Boy*

Another from the Sasha Fierce album, If I Were a Boy, speaks of a female protagonist who processes her difficult breakup by imagining a gender swap, fantasizing about how she would act if she were a man —the lyrics indict bad male behavior rather than celebrate it.

The pop and RnB ballad features strong acoustic guitar, heavy drums, and strings. Set to a moderate 90 BPM tempo, the song heavily features chords that are evident on the kalimba notation.

- CCDEG

GGAGFE

CCCDE EFED CEEEFEDCC

CCDEG

GAGFE

C EEEEFED

CDEEFEDCC

EFFFCD

C°C°D°E°G°

G°G°G°A°G°F°E°

C°D°E° E° E° F° E°D°C°

C° E° E° E° F° E° D° D° C°

92: Despacito – Luis Fonsi ft Daddy Yankee

Despacito was released in January 2017, with Puerto Rican artist Luis Fonzi, featuring fellow Puerto Rican rapper Daddy Yankee.

The song is a reggaeton and Latin pop set to 89 BPM and set to B minor.

The song describes a desire by the protagonist to have a smooth and romantic sexual relationship with someone.

The remix, released in April 2017, featured Canadian pop star, Justin Bieber and he helped push the song to new heights, pushing it to number in many countries worldwide.

Kalimba Songbook

- Letter notes

C° B A E E A A G A F

F A A B C° G C° C° D° D° B

C° B A E E A A G A F

F A A B C° G G C° C° D° D° B

E° E° D° E° E° F° F° C° C° F° F° G° F° E°

C° E° E° F° E° D°

E° E° D° E° E° F° F° C° C° F° F° G° F° E°

C° E° E° F° E° D°

C° B A E

Number notation

1° 7 6 3 3 6 6 5 6 4

4 6 6 7 1° 5 1° 1° 2° 2° 7

1° 7 6 3 3 6 6 5 6 4

4 6 6 7 1° 5 5 1° 1° 2° 2° 7

3° 3° 2° 3° 3° 4° 4° 1° 1° 4° 4° 5° 4° 3°

3° 2°

3° 3° 2° 3° 3° 4° 4° 1° 1° 4° 4° 5° 4° 3°

1° 3° 3° 4° 3° 2°

1° 7 6 3

Celine Dion

Celine Dion is known for her powerful and moving love ballads that blend well with her powerful vocals, making her one of the most successful artists of all time.

Dion has sold over 200 million records, making her one of the most successful artists ever.

Some of her songs on the Kalimba are.

93: *My Heart Will Go On*

My Heart Will Go On was composed as the soundtrack for the major hit film Titanic.

Released in December 1997, the song was a global hit, topping charts in several countries worldwide, and is one of the best-selling songs in physical copy ever, with over 18 million copies sold.

The strong is heavy on instrumentals, featuring strings and rhythm guitars, with Celine Dion's vocal providing the emotional depth of the instrumentals.

- Kalimba Notes

1′ 2′ 3′ / 2′ 1′ 2′ 5′ / 4′ 3′ 1′ / 6 5

1′ 2′ 3′ / 4′ 3′ 2′ 1′ 3′ 2′ 5′ / 3′ 5′ 6′ / 5′ 3′ 2′

1′ 1′ / 1′ 7 1′ / 1′ 7 1′ / 2′ 3′ 2′

1′ 1′ / 1′ 7 1′ / 1′ 5

1′ 1′ / 1′ 7 1′ / 1′ 7 1′ / 2′ 3′ 2′

1′ 1′ / 1′ 7 1′ / 1′ 5

1′ 2′ 5 5′ 4′ 3′ 2′

3′ 4′ 3′ 2′ 1′ 7 1′ 7 7 6 5

1′ 2′ 5 5′ 4′ 3′ 2′

3′ 4′ 3′ 2′ 1′ 7 1′ 1′ 7 1′ 2′ 3′ 2′ 1′

1′ 2′ 3′ / 2′ 1′ 2′ 5′ / 4′ 3′ 1′ / 6 5

1' 2' 3' / 4' 3' 2' 1' 3' 2' 5' / 3' 5' 6' / 5' 3' 2'

1' 2' 5 5' 4' 3' 2'

3' 4' 3' 2' 1' 7 1' 7 7 6 5

1' 2' 5 5' 4' 3' 2'

3' 4' 3' 2' 1' 7 1' 1' 7 1' 2' 3' 2' 1'

94: *Immortality*

Immortality, released in 1998, is of Celine Dion's 1997 album, *Let's Talk About Love*.

Dion featured the Bee Gees (of Stayin' Alive), and the song got off to positive reception, climbing into the top ten charts in several countries.

The strong mostly features piano, though heavy drums and guitar come in during the climax, with the Bee Gees providing haunting background vocals.

Immortality

13531'353

13531'3531

5' 5' 4' 4' 3' (3'-1) (3 53 1'3531)

3' (3'-3) 5 (1) 2' 1' (1-1) (3 53 1'3531)

4' 4' 3' 3' 2' 2' (246)

51' 2' 3' 4' 3'2' 2' (246)

1' 1' 3' 5' 1" (7' 5-7) (6'-6) (5'-5) 6' (5' 5-7)

(6-1) 1' 4' 6' (1'-3'-5' 5) 3'6 4' (3'3-5)

5 1'2' 3' 3' (2' 1' 5) (246)

3' 3' 2' 1' 3' 5' 1" (7' 5-7) (6'-6) (5'-5) 6' (5' 5-7)

6 (6-1) 1' 4' 6' (1'-3'-5' 5) 3' 6 4' (3' 3-5)

51' 2' 3' 3' (2' 1' 5) (246)

(5'-5) (1-1) 5'4' (3'3-5) (3'-3) (5'-5) 3'2' (1'-1)

1' 2' 3' 21' 3' 2' 2' (246)

(3'3-5) (4' 4-6) (5' 5-7) 5' (4' 4-6)

(1-3-5) 3'3' 3' (4' 4-6) 4' 4' 4' (5' 5-7) 5' (4' 4-6)

(1-3-5) 3'3' 3' (4' 4-6) 4' 4' 4' (5' 5-7) 5' (4' 4-6)

3' 3'2' 1'(5-7-2')

5' (5'-5) (1-1) 5' 4' (3' 3-5) (3'-3) (5'-5) 3' 2' (1'-1)

1'2'3' 2' 1' (5-7-2) 1'2 3'2' 1' (5-7-2')

2'3'2'1' (5-1) (351')

(5'-5) (5-5) (4-4) (4-4) 3 (3' 1-3-5)

Britney Spears

American Singer Britney Spears is often credited with reviving teen pop in the late 90s and early 2000s.

As a pop icon, Britney has sold over 150 million records worldwide, with her songs hitting cultural milestones as they remain widely beloved and covered.

Below we look at some of them on the Kalimba.

95: *Everytime*

Everytime is off Britney's 4th studio album, *In the Zone*, released in 2003.

The song is a pop ballad with the protagonist pleading with a former lover for forgiveness.

Everytime was widely praised for its lyrics and composition and was a hit in several countries, climbing into the top ten in charts.

Set to a tempo of 110 BPM, Everytime features a strong piano accompaniment to Spear's vocals.

- Numbers:

$1\,3\,5$

$(1°3°)\,1°\,2°\,2\,5\,3$

$1\,3\,5$

$(1°3°)\,1°\,7\,2\,5$

$1\,3\,5$

$(1°3°)\,1°\,2°\,2\,5\,3$

$1\,3\,5$

$(1°3°)\,1°\,7\,2\,1°\,7\,6$

$1\,3\,5$

$(1°3°)\,1°\,2°\,2\,5\,3$

$1\,3\,5$

$(1°3°)\,1°\,7\,2\,1°\,7\,6$

$3\,5$

$7\,(33°)\,7\,1°\,1$

$5\,3$

$1\,3\,7\,(33°)\,7\,1°\,1$

$1°\,2°\,3°$

$1\,3$

$5°\,5°\,(55°)\,3°\,2°\,2$

$5\,(35)\,3°\,4°\,(33°)$

$3°\,3°\,5\,1°\,7\,2$

$7\,(57)\,5\,6\,1$

$6\,(46)\,1°$

7 (33°) 7 1° 1

5 3

1 3

7 (33°) 7 1° 1

1° 2° 3°

1 3

5° 5° (55°) 3° 2° 2

5 (35) 3° 4° (33°)

3° 3° 5 1° 7 2

7 (57) 5 6 1

6 (46) 1°

(27) 5 7 1° 2°

1 3

5° 5° (55°) 3° 2° 2

5 (35) 3° 4° (33°)

3° 3° 5 1° 7 2

7 (57) 5 6 1

6 (46) 1°

(27) 5 7 1° 2°

(461°)

6° 6 (55°) 3° (22°) 5

1° 3° 3 4° 3° 2°

5 7 1° 2° 3°

(461°)

6° 6 (55°) 3° (22°) 5
1° 3° 3 4° 3° 2°
6° 7° 1°° 7° 6°
1°° 7° (5°7°) 6°

.....

Letters:

C E G

(C°E°) C° D° D G E

C E G

(C°E°) C° B D G

C E G

(C°E°) C° D° D G E

C E G

(C°E°) C° B D C° B A

C E G

(C°E°) C° D° D G E

C E G

(C°E°) C° B D C° B A

E G

B (EE°) B C° C

G E

C E B (EE°) B C° C

C° D° E°

C E
G° G ° (GG°) E° D° D
G (EG) E° F° (EE°)
E° E° G C° B D
B (GB) G A C
A (FA) C°
(DB) G B C° D°
C E
G° G° (GG°) E° D° D
G (EG) E° F° (EE°)
E° E° G C° B D
B (GB) G A C
A (FA) C°
(DB) G B C° D°
C E G
(C°E°) C° D° D
G E
C E G
(C°E°) C° B D G
C E
C° (EE°) C° D° D
G E
C E
C° (EE°) C° B C° B A

C E

C° C° (EE°) C°

E° E F° E° D°

C E G

(C°E°) C° B D° C° B D

E G

B (EE°) B C° C

G E

C E

B (EE°) B C° C

C° D° E°

C E

G° G° (GG°) E° D° D

G (EG) E° F° (EE°)

E° E° G C° B D

B (GB) G A C

A (FA) C°

(DB) G B C° D°

C E

G° G° (GG°) E° D° D

G (EG) E° F° (EE°)

E° E° G C° B D

B (GB) G A C

A (FA) C°

(DB) G B C° D°

(FAC°)

A° A (GG°) E° (DD°) G

C° E° E F° E° D°

G B C° D° E°

(FAC°)

A° A (GG°) E° (DD°) G

C° E° E F° E° D°

A° B° C°° B° A°

C°° B° (G°B°) A°

.....

96: Toxic

Another hit from *In the Zone* album, Toxic features strong drums and guitar accompaniments, with high-pitched Bollywood instrumentals in the background.

The song topped charts in countless countries and was considered the album's best track.

The Dance-pop is set to 143 BPM and tuned to C Major. As shown below, you can capture its disorienting charm on the Kalimba.

- 6 6 1° 7 6 7 1° 6 1° 7 6

3°° 7° 1°° 7° 6°

6 6 1° 7 6 7 1° 6 1° 7 6

3°° 7° 1°° 7° 6°

6 6 1° 7 6 7 1° 6 1° 7 6

3°° 7° 1°° 7° 6°

6 6 1° 7 6 7 1° 6 1° 7 6

3°° 7° 1°° 7° 6°

6 7 1° 7 6

6 6 1° 6 1°/6 6 1° 7 6

6 6 6 6 1° 6 1°/1 5 7 6 5

3 3 5 3 5

6 6 1° 7 6 7 1° 6 1° 7 6

3°° 7° 1°° 7° 6°

6 7 1° 7 6

6 6 1° 6 1°/6 6 1° 7 6

6 6 6 1° 6 1°/1 5 7 6 5

3 3 5 3 5

6 6 1° 7 6 7 1° 6 1° 7 6

3°° 7° 1°° 7° 6°

6 3° 5°

6/5° 2°° 5° 3°

6 3° 3° 3° 5° 5° 5°

6/5° 2°° 5° 3°

1

3 2° 3° 5° 3° 2°

6 6 1° 7 6 7 1° 6 1° 7 6

3°° 7° 1°° 7° 6°

6 6 6 6 6 6 6 6

6 6 6 6 6 3° 5°

6/7° 6° 5° 5° 6/3°

1/2° 1° 5° 1

7 /6° 3° 7/6°

2/3° 6° 6° 3° 2/6°

6/7° 6° 5° 5° 6/3°

1/2° 1° 5° 1/6 1°

4/3° 2° 1° 1° 4/6 1°

3/3° 2° 1° 7/2° 3°

6 6 5 6 3°

1/1° 1/6 1°

7/3° 2° 1° 1° 6 1°

2/3° 2° 1° 2° 2/3°

6 6° 3°

1/1° 1

6 6 1° 7 6 7 1° 6 1° 7 6

3°° 7° 1°° 7° 6°

6 1° 7 6

6 6 1° 6 1°/6 6 1° 7 6

6 6 6 1° 6 1°/1 5 7 6 5

3 3 3 5 3 5

6 6 1° 7 6 7 1° 6 1° 7 6

6° 1°° 7° 3°°

6 3° 5°

6/5° 2°° 5° 3°

6 3° 3° 3° 5° 5° 5°

6/5° 2°° 5° 3°

1

3 2° 3° 5° 3° 2°

6 6 1° 7 6 7 1° 6 1° 7 6

3°° 7° 1°° 7° 6°

6 6 6 6 6 6 6 6

6 6 6 6 6 3° 5°

6/7° 6° 5° 5° 6/3°

1/2° 1° 5° 1

7 /6° 3° 7/6°

2/3° 6° 6° 3° 2/6°

6/7° 6° 5° 5° 6/3°

1/2° 1° 5° 1/6 1°

4/3° 2° 1° 1° 4/6 1°

3/3° 2° 1° 7/2° 3°

6 5 6 3°

1/1° 1/6 1°

7/3° 2° 1° 1° 6 1°

2/3° 2° 1° 2° 2/3°

6 6° 3°

1/1° 1

6 6 1° 7 6 7 1° 6 6 1°

3/3° 2° 1° 7/2° 3°

6/3°°

1/3°° 1°°

7/6°

2

6/3°°

1/3°° 1°°

4/6°

3

6 6

6 6

7° 6° 5° 5° 3°

2° 1° 5°

7 /6° 3° 7/6°

2/3° 6° 6° 3° 2/6°

6/7° 6° 5° 5° 6/3°

1/2° 1° 5° 1/6 1°

4/3° 2° 1° 1° 4/6 1°

3/3° 2° 1° 7/2° 3° 5°

6/7° 6° 5° 5° 6/3°

1/2° 1° 5° 1

7 /6° 3° 7/6°

2/3° 6° 6° 3° 2/6°

6/7° 6° 5° 5° 6/3°

1/2° 1° 5° 1/6 1°

4/3° 2° 1° 1° 4/6 1°

3/3° 2° 1° 7/2° 3°

6 6 1° 6 1° 6 1°

1 /1° 6 1° 6 1/1°

7 6 1° 6 1° 6 1°

2/6 1° 6 1° 6 2/1°

6 6 1° 6 1° 6 1°

1 /1° 6 1° 6 1/1°

4/6 1° 6 1° 6 1°

3/3°° 7° 1°° 7° 6°

97: Sia – Snowman

Sia started her music career in the mid-90s but got worldwide recognition in 2014.

Snowman is off her eighth studio album, *Everyday Is Christmas*, released in 2017.

The song features a piano and guitar, with Sia's strong vocal performances carrying through the song.

Numbered Notation:

1 3 5 1° 5 3 1 3 5 1° 5 3

1 3 5 1° 3° 5° 1°°

6 (461°3°) 2° 4 6 3° 2° 2° 4

(2572°) 5 2° 3° 2° 5 2° 3° 2° 5 2°

3° (62°) 3 1° 1 3 6 1°

2° 3° (62°) 3 1° 1 3 6 1°

6 (461°3°) 2° 4 6 3° 2° 2° 4

(2572°) 5 2° 3° 2° 5 2° 3° 2° 5 2°

3° (62°) 3 1° 1 3 6 1°

2° 3° (62°) 3 1° 7° 6° 3° 1°

4 3 5 7 3° 3 7 (61°) 2° 1° 7 6 6

(25) 7 2° 4° 5 2° (3°1) 4° 3° 2° 1° 7

3 5 7 3° 3 7 (61°) 2° 1° 7 6 6

(3°1) 2° (24°) 3°

(15) 6 1° 3° 1° 5 (46) 1° 3° 2° 1°

(15) 6 1° 3° 1° 5 (46) 1° 3° 2° 1°

(15) 6 1° 3° 1° 5 (46) 1° 3° 2° 1°

(15) 6 1° 3° 1° 5 (46) 1° 3° 2° 1°

1° (3°1) 1° 5 2° (27) 5 7 1° (46) 1 4 6 1° 4° 4
1° (3°1) 1° 5 2° (27) 5 7 1° (46) 1 4 6 1° 4° 4
1 3 5 1° 5 3 1 3 5 1° 5 3
1 3 5 1° 3° 5° 1°°

Lettered Notation:

C E G C° G E C E G C° G E

C E G C° E° G° C°°

A (FAC°E°) D° F A E° D° D° F

(DGBD°) G D° E° D° G D° E° D° G D°

E° (AD°) E C° C E A C°

D° E° (AD°) E C° C E A C°

A (FAC°E°) D° F A E° D° D° F

(DGBD°) G D° E° D° G D° E° D° G D°

E° (AD°) E C° C E A C°

D° E° (AD°) E C° B° A° E° C°

F E G B E° E B (AC°) D° C° B A A

(DG) B D° F° G D° (E°C) F° E° D° C° B

E G B E° E B (AC°) D° C° B A A

(E°C) D° (DF°) E°

(CG) A C° E° C° G (FA) C° E° D° C°

(CG) A C° E° C° G (FA) C° E° D° C°

(CG) A C° E° C° G (FA) C° E° D° C°

(CG) A C° E° C° G (FA) C° E° D° C°

C° (E°C) C° G D° (DB) G B C° (FA) C F A C° F° F

C° (E°C) C° G D° (DB) G B C° (FA) C F A C° F° F

C E G C° G E C E G C° G E

C E G C° E° G° C°°

98: Melanie Martinez – Cry Baby

Cry Baby is a song by American singer, Melanie Martinez who started her career in 2012.

Cry Baby is the lead song from her debut album of the same name, released in 2015.

The track is alternative pop with minimalist electronics instrumentals that provide the spooky feeling.

Set to a tempo of 95 BPM, the song is set in F minor.

-

F-FGA D-D D F x3

G-GAB G-CCG

CF-F C D-F ECBFB D-B C

CF-F C D-F ECB (G-B) B (C-B) G

GF-FC D-F ECB F-B B D-B C

CF-BCCBD C-G BA-C C

FABC-DAABBF

ABC-DAABF

ACABAGAGAG

FFABC-DAABBF

A-DCA ABB (A-F)

C-D EABAGAGA-CG

CBAB-D CBA B-DCBAF

FFGF-ABC

B-E CB AB B-ECBAB

ABAB-BAF

B-D CBA B-DC BAF

FFGF-ABC

B-E B B-E CA B-B BBCA

F-F GA D-DD FX3

G-G AB G-CCG F-F|

99: *Game of Thrones Theme Song*

Game of Thrones is one of the most popular TV shows. The drama series, which ran for eight full seasons, is about power and politics to claim the throne. With such heavy themes, the series needed a strong theme song. The theme song, composed in 2011, does not disappoint.

Ramin Djawadi, the composer, used a cello as the lead instrument, giving the theme song a rich, fantastical feel.

The song has become popular among instrumentalists, covered widely and on the Kalimba; you can play it as shown below:

- 3' 6 1' 2' 3' 6 1' 2' 7

3 5 6 7 / 3 5 6 7 / 3 5 6 7

2' 5 1' 7 2' 5 1' 7 6

3 4 5 6 / 3 4 5 6 / 3 4 5 6

3' 6 1' 2' 3' 6 / 1' 2' 3' 6 / 1' 2' 3' 6 / 1' 2' 7

3 5 6 7 / 3 5 6 7 / 3 5 6 7

2' 5 1' 7 2' 5 / 1' 7 2' 5 / 1' 7 2' 5 / 1' 7 6

3 4 5 6 / 3 4 5 6 / 3 4 5 6

3' 6 1' 2' 3' 6 1' 2' 7

3 5 6 7 / 3 5 6 7 / 3 5 6 7

2' 5 7 1' 7 5 6

3 4 5 6 / 3 4 5 6 / 3 4 5 6

Game of Thrones Theme Song

EA CDE A CDB

DG CBD G CBA

EA CDE A CDB

DGB CB GA

EA CDE A CDE A CDE A CDB

EGAB EGAB EGAB

DG CBD G CBD G CBD G CBA

EFGA EFGA EFGA

EA CDE A CDE A CDE A CDB

EGAB EGAB EGAB

DG CBD G CBD G CBD G CBA

EFGA EFGA EFGA

A AA GAG ECA FF EFE CAF

CC D E

A AA GAG ECA FF EFE CAF

CC B A

EFGA EFGA EFGA

100: Red Velvet – Psycho

Red Velvet is a South Korean pop girl band.

Their song, Psycho, is one of their most successful singles. Released in 2017, Psycho is off their third studio album, *The ReVe Festival: Finale.*

The RnB track features strong trap and future bass elements and has classical strings.

- 1° 2° ° 2° 3° 5° 3°

5 1° 2° 1° 2° 3° 7 7

5 5 4° 4° 4° 4° 3° 6

4° 4° 4° 4° 3 6

6° 5° 4° 3° 2° 2° 2° 2° 1° 5

1° 2° 1° 2° 3° 5° 3°

5 1° 2° 1° 2° 3° 7 7

4° 4° 4° 4° 3 6

4° 4° 4° 4° 3 6

6° 5° 4° 3° 2° 2° 2°

1° 2° 1° 2° 3° 1°° 2°° 3°° 3°° 1°° 5° 7° 1°°

5° 7° 7° 7° 7° 7° 6° 1°° 2° 3° 2°

5° 7° 7° 7° 7° 7° 6° 1°°

1° 2° 1° 2° 1° 2° 1° 3° 2° 3° 2°

1° 2° 1° 2° 1° 2° 1° 3° 2° 3° 2°

1° 3° 3° 3° 4° 5° 5° 3° 2° 1°

3° 4° 5° 6° 5° 4° 5°

4° 3° 1° 4° 3°

1° 4° 3° 2° 4° 3°

2° 1° 3° 2° 3° 2°

1° 2° 1° 2° 1° 2° 1° 3° 2° 3° 2°

1° 3° 3° 3° 4° 5° 5° 3° 2° 1°

3° 4° 5° 6° 5° 4° 5°

4° 3° 1° 4° 3°

1° 4° 3° 2° 4° 3°

C° D° C D E° G° E°

G C D° C

D E° B B

A° G F

E

D° Do Do D° C° G

C D

C

D

E° G° E°

G G F F F Fo E° A

F F F Fo E° A

A° G F

E° D° D° D°

C° D° C

D E° C°°°°°°°

E°°C°°G B°C°°

G°B B B B B°A°C D°E D°

G°B B B B B°A°C°°

C°D°C°D°C D°C°E'D°E'D°

C°D°C D C D

E°D°E D°

C E E E F G°G°E D°C°

E°F G A G F G°

F°E°C°F°E°

C°F°E D°F°E°

D°C°E D°E D°

C°D°C°D°C°D° E°D°E°D°

C°E°E E°F G°G°E°D°C°

E°F G A G F°G°

F°E°C°F°E°

C°F°E D°F°E°|

Conclusion

Playing musical instruments is often a very fulfilling venture. The Kalimba is among the easiest instruments you can lay your hands on and play.

The wide range of music we have covered provides an insight into the versatility of the simple yet very effective music instrument.

Although the instrument can only play on one scale (a diatonic instrument), the various ways you can tune its keys means you can find your way through several songs.

Thus, I hope you find the above 100 songs great to get you going in your new kalimba playing hobby.

PS: I'd like your feedback. If you are happy with this book, please leave a review on Amazon.

Please leave a review for this book on Amazon by visiting the page below:

https://amzn.to/2VMR5qr

Made in the USA
Monee, IL
15 December 2024